ANCHOR
COMPLETE
EMBROIDERY
COURSE

ANCHOR
COMPLETE
EMBROIDERY
COURSE

Christina Marsh

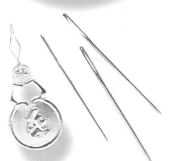

David & Charles

A DAVID & CHARLES BOOK

First published in the UK in 1998

A catalogue record for this book is available from the British Library.

ISBN 0 7153 0717 7

Designed and typeset by Fiona Roberts at
The Design Revolution, Brighton
and printed in Great Britain
by Butler & Tanner Ltd
for David & Charles
Brunel House • Newton Abbot • Devon

CONTENTS

INTRODUCTION

Embroidery is enjoying a revival and new generations are discovering just how easy it is to create beautiful embroideries that are both enjoyable and relaxing to stitch.

If you are a beginner or new to embroidery you will find all the information and help you need in this book. Learn each stitch by following the fully illustrated step-by-step instructions. As you work through the book look for the boxes which contain handy hints and advice.

The very first project chapter, Just Five Stitches, has been especially created for beginners. It contains five basic stitches to get you started together with a practice sampler and a host of other fun projects.

The stitches in this book have been divided into five family groups, each containing six of the most popular stitches. Each stitch is clearly explained and illustrated and you can try out all six by making the pretty practice sampler which accompanies each stitch family. Alternatively, choose one of the other delightful projects built around that particular stitch family.

As you grow in confidence you will want to branch out and create more individualistic projects. The final chapter, Mix & Match, shows how you can change fabric and threads, create new colour schemes and extend your design skills. Whether you are a beginner or a more advanced stitcher you will find there is plenty of practical help and suggestions for extending and personalising your embroidery. The projects in this book are just right, whether you are stitching for yourself, your family or your home.

CHAPTER ONE

GETTING STARTED

f you are new to embroidery – or if you are in need of a refresher course –
you'll find this chapter invaluable. It contains information about the basic
materials you need, including fabrics, threads and embroidery frames, details on
transferring your chosen design to the fabric and basic stitch instructions. When
you've completed your embroidery you'll want to know how to display
it effectively, so there's also information on framing.

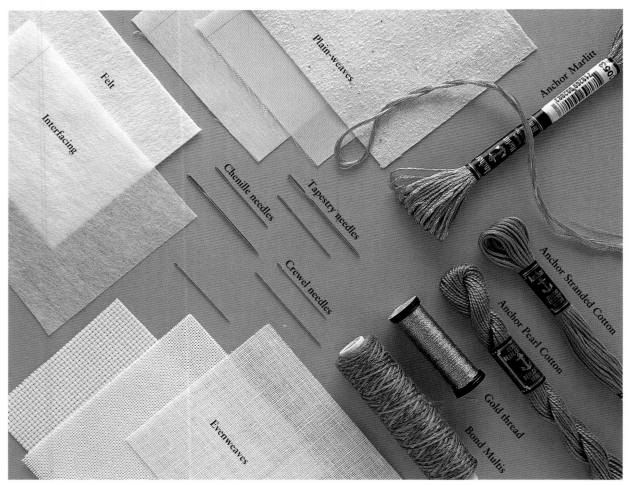

Here is a selection of fabrics, threads and needles available for embroidery. You can work on plain-weave
fabrics (top), evenweaves (bottom left) or even felt backed with interfacing (top left).

MATERIALS & EQUIPMENT

There is a vast array of material and equipment available for embroidery, and this can sometimes be overwhelming for the beginner, not knowing exactly what to buy. The following information lists the basic materials and equipment you may need and forms a practical guide for anyone new to surface embroidery.

FABRICS FOR EMBROIDERY

These can be grouped under two headings: evenweave fabrics and plain-weave fabrics. *Evenweave fabrics* have a regular weave with an exact number of threads in each direction. These are easy to count, making it straightforward to create stitches of an even size and spacing. This makes them ideal for beginners. Evenweave fabrics come in various grades, identified by the number of threads to the inch – the fabric count. (The count is usually calculated to the inch, even in countries which generally use metric measurements.) The higher the count the more threads there are to the inch, and the smaller your stitches will be. Conversely, the lower the count the fewer threads and the larger your stitches will be.

Plain-weave fabrics, which include home-furnishing fabrics as well as dressmaking materials, can be made of natural or synthetic fibres and may be smooth or textured. The most useful fabric under this heading is plain cotton which is both the easiest to apply a transfer to and to stitch on. Non-stretch synthetic materials can also be used but they require a backing such as iron-on interfacing or light-weight cotton. It is possible to use stretchy synthetics (with a backing) but it is not recommended.

Backing fabric should be used under the surface layer to prevent puckering except with small projects, when this isn't really necessary, especially if you are stitching on medium-weight cotton. Use light-weight cotton as a backing for evenweave fabrics, such as 28-count Linda and 28/32-count Irish linen, and for both natural and synthetic plain-weave fabrics. Alternatively, with smooth synthetics you can use iron-on interfacing instead of a separate backing.

FABRIC ALLOWANCE

The exact quantity of fabric required for a project is listed at the beginning of each project. However, you will need to allow sufficient fabric to fit your embroidery frame. When using small and medium-size circular hoops allow 10cm (4in) more than the size of the hoop; for a large hoop allow 15cm (6in). With stretchers the fabric should touch all four sides of the frame and with roller frames the fabric should be long enough to attach to the webbing (at the top and bottom of the frame).

THREADS

There is a wonderful array of threads available for embroidery in stunning colour ranges. You can use just one type, such as stranded cotton, or combine different threads to produce breathtaking projects. Throughout the book thread options are given for many projects and in the Mix & Match chapter (page 113) you will learn how to change the threads for a project to suit a particular colour scheme you have in mind. Here is a list of the threads used in this book, which is just a selection of the types available.

Anchor Stranded Cotton This lustrous thread consists of six strands which can be used as it is, stranded or blended with other colours or different thread types, depending on the effects desired and the count of the fabric.

Anchor Pearl Cotton This twisted cotton comes in three different thicknesses: 3, 5 and 8, and should be used as it comes.

Bond Multis This variegated, twisted embellishment yarn comes in a range of exciting colours.

Anchor Marlitt This high-gloss rayon thread consists of four strands which can be used as it is, stranded or blended with other colours or different types of thread, depending on the effect required.

Gold threads These range from single-strand thread in different thicknesses and textures to multi-stranded thread which can be used as it comes or divided into strands.

NEEDLES

Needles for embroidery divide into two main groups: sharp-pointed or blunt-ended needles. Sharp-pointed needles are suited to closely woven fabrics and blunt-ended ones to evenweave fabrics such as Aida. Increasingly needles are sold in selection packs, so when choosing a needle select one with an eye large enough to thread with ease which is the right size and thickness for your fabric. The needle should pass smoothly through the fabric without the need for tugging and pulling as this could spoil your finished embroidery and make stitching difficult.

Crewel needles These have a sharp point and large eye and are suitable for most types of embroidery. They come in sizes 1 to 10; the higher the size, the finer the needle.

Chenille needles These have a larger eye and sharp point. They are mainly used for thicker threads and fabric and come in sizes 14 to 26. These needles are not used in this book.

Tapestry needles These have a large eye and a blunt end which glides smoothly between the threads without splitting them. This makes them ideal for stitching on evenweave fabrics, such as Aida, as they do not damage the threads. They come in sizes 14 to 26.

Sharps and betweens These general-purpose sewing needles are used for all tacking and hand finishing.

FRAMES

Embroidery should always be worked in a frame as this helps to reduce puckering. There are two basic types of frame: circular and rectangular. Circular frames, such as tambours and flexi-hoops, come in a wide range of sizes. Rectangular frames, such as roller frames (slate) and stretchers, are also available in different sizes but they tend to be larger than hoops. In a circular frame the fabric is trapped between two hoops and on a rectangular frame the work is attached to the edges. (For more details see pages 20-23.)

SUPPORT EQUIPMENT

There are a few additional pieces of equipment you will require or may find useful. For example, depending on which method you choose to transfer your design to the fabric, you may need a soluble pen, transfer pencil, tracing paper or dressmakers' carbon paper. You may also need some basic dressmaking equipment, such as scissors, a tape measure, pins and possibly a thimble. For fine work you may find an embroiderer's magnifier useful.

PREPARING & TRANSFERRING DESIGNS

Before the fabric is mounted in a frame and stitching can commence, you generally need to transfer your design to the centre of your fabric. The exception is with fabrics for counted-thread embroidery such as Aida when you can work straight from a chart or photograph. There are numerous transfer techniques, but in this chapter you'll find details on four of the most popular methods. Each technique is illustrated with step-by-step photography and is accompanied by simple instructions. For a quick-reference guide to the pros and cons of each method, see the verdict box in the corner of each page. If you are new to surface embroidery, study all the techniques before selecting a method.

A photocopier provides the easiest way of enlarging or reducing a design.

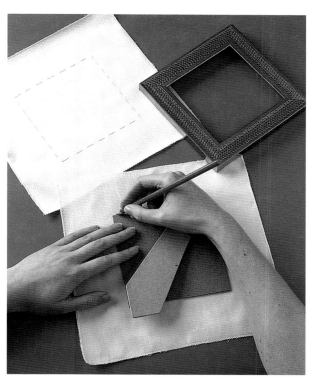

Mounting work in a frame is easier if the outline is marked and tacked.

ALTERING THE DESIGN SIZE

A design can easily be enlarged or reduced by photocopying the original for your own use. The thread instructions will remain the same for small adjustments, but if you enlarge a design by more than twice its original size you may need to adjust the thread thickness or even change the stitch. All the projects in this book require less than one skein of thread in each colour, but if you enlarge the design greatly you may need more.

PREPARING YOUR FABRIC

If you intend to frame your finished embroidery, prepare the fabric by tacking around the frame edges as explained here. The tacked line is a useful guide both for centring your design and for lacing the finished work (see page 28). Lay out the fabric, wrong-side up, and centre the backing board on top. Draw round the board with a pencil, then work over the drawn line with tacking stitches. Turn the fabric right-side up.

Using a Soluble Pen

1 *Assembling your materials* Set out a transfer pen, masking tape, a tracing of the design, fabric and a lightbox. (A window is a good substitute for a lightbox.) There are two types of transfer pen – air-soluble pens which leave a mark which should vanish over time and needs redrawing if left for too long, and water-soluble pens which are removed by dampening the fabric.

VERDICT

SOLUBLE PENS

✓ *Soluble pens are very easy to use.*

✓ *They produce a bright, clear outline which is easy to see.*

✗ *The lines from air-soluble pens disappear within hours and the outline may need redrawing if the project is not stitched quickly.*

✗ *The lines from water-soluble pens do not always disappear on all types of fabric – it is advisable to do a test strip first.*

Soluble pens are easy to use and produce a very clear outline. However, the line can disappear too quickly with air-soluble pens and be hard to remove with water-soluble pens. It is always advisable to cover the outline completely when stitching.

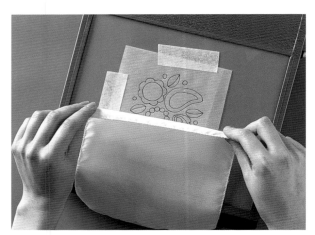

2 *Preparing the work for tracing* If you have used a pencil to trace the design go over the line with a black felt pen to produce a stronger outline. Tape the tracing the right way up onto the lightbox or window. Tape the fabric, right-side up, on top. If you have prepared your fabric for a frame with tacking, make sure your design is centred between the tacked lines.

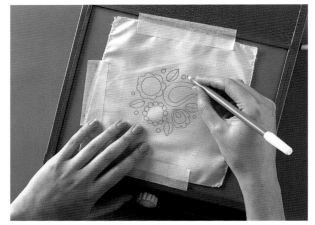

3 *Tracing the design lines* Use the tip of the soluble pen to trace the lines of the design onto the fabric. Follow the lines carefully as you may not be able to remove wrongly drawn lines later. Although the marks from soluble pens do disappear from most fabrics they are not equally successful on all fabrics, so it is advisable to cover all the lines completely when stitching.

Using a Transfer Pencil

1 ***Tracing the design*** Set out your design, tracing paper, masking tape, fabric, a pencil and transfer pencil. Check the size of the design before tracing – if an adjustment is required enlarge or reduce the motif with a photocopier. Tape the tracing paper over the motif and then use a sharp pencil to trace the design.

2 ***Applying the transfer pencil*** Turn the tracing paper to the wrong side and retrace the outline with a transfer pencil. As this requires a firm pressure it should be done on a hard surface. Always make sure the pencil has a sharp point as tracing with a blunt pencil will result in thick lines which may be difficult to cover when stitching.

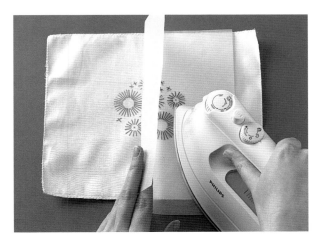

3 ***Ironing the transfer*** Place the tracing over the fabric so that the side with the transfer pencil is face down on the fabric. Use a hot iron and press down on the transfer – this needs to be done with care as any movement could result in a blurred edge to the transferred image. This technique does not work on all fibres so it is advisable to do a test strip first.

VERDICT

TRANSFER PENCIL

✔ *A transfer pencil is inexpensive and lasts a long time.*

✔ *It is simple to use.*

✔ *It works well on felt.*

✘ *A very hot iron is required which is unsuitable for certain fabrics, such as synthetics.*

✘ *Moving the tracing when ironing it can blur the image.*

✘ *The pencil does not work on all types of fabric so it is advisable to do a test strip.*

A transfer pencil is easy to use but it does not always produce a strong, clear image. However, faded lines can be strengthened by retracing with a pencil. This technique is generally not suitable for delicate fabrics.

Using Dressmakers' Carbon

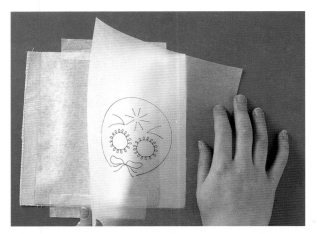

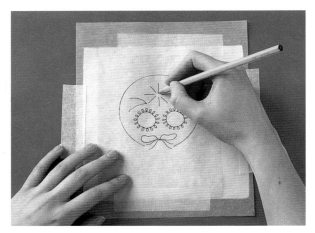

1 *Preparing your materials* Set out your fabric, dressmakers' carbon, a tracing of the motif, masking tape and a sharp pencil. Tape the fabric right-side up onto a firm, smooth surface and place the carbon paper coloured side down on the fabric. Tape the traced design on top.

2 *Tracing the design* Make sure that each layer in the sandwich is secure and will not move during the tracing. Trace over the design, applying a firm, even pressure but not so firm that you tear the traced design. Uneven pressure can result in varying line strength.

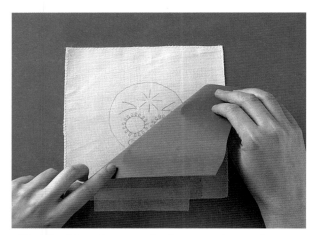

3 *Checking the transfer* Remove the tracing and carbon to reveal the motif. If the pressure on the pencil has been uneven you may find some lines are fainter than others. Lightly retrace any faint lines on the fabric with an ordinary pencil. Carbon rubs off, so it is not suitable for large embroidery projects.

VERDICT

DRESSMAKERS' CARBON

✔ Carbon paper is easy to use.

✔ It comes in a range of colours.

✘ The outline can be uneven if the pressure on the pencil is varied when tracing.

✘ The carbon is easily rubbed off.

Dressmakers' carbon is easy to use and because it comes in a wide range of colours it is ideal for tracing on coloured fabrics where a contrasting colour is required. Faint lines can be reinforced with an ordinary pencil. However, dressmakers' carbon is not suitable for textured fabrics, large projects or those that take a long time to stitch as the carbon rubs off.

Using Tacking

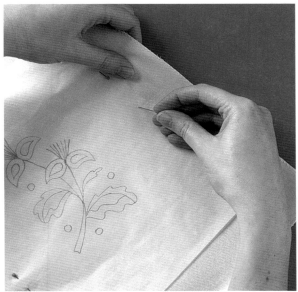

1 *Tracing the design* Lay out your fabric, pins, a sharp-pointed needle and sewing cotton. Trace your motif onto tissue-grade paper which tears easily. Make sure your tracing is large enough to cover the embroidery when framed. Pin the tracing right-side up on the fabric.

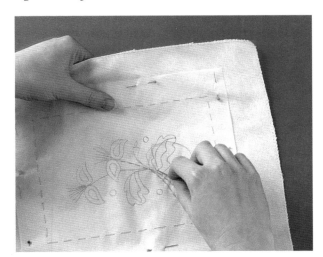

2 *Tacking the design* Thread a sharp-pointed needle with ordinary sewing cotton in a bright colour for the tacking. Knot the end of the cotton. Start with the knot at the top of the work and tack by stitching a line of small running stitches along all the lines of the design.

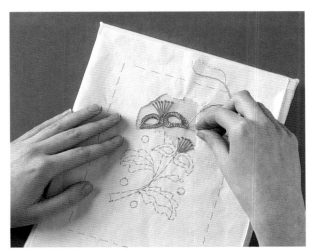

3 *Removing the tracing paper* Gradually remove the tracing paper and the tacking line as you embroider. If you have difficulty in following the outline when the tacking is removed retrace it lightly with a pencil. The tracing paper protects areas still to be embroidered.

WORKING WITH A PATTERN

All the projects in this book are worked on closely woven fabrics or evenweaves. Projects stitched on Aida fabric can be worked directly from a chart (see Working from a Chart, page 18) but for all other fabrics you will need to transfer the design to the fabric using the full-size pattern provided with each project. To stitch the embroidery refer to the numbers and letters on the pattern and use the accompanying key to identify them. The thread colour is indicated by a number and the stitch by a letter. The fine dotted lines indicate the direction of the stitch.

PROJECT INSTRUCTIONS

If you wish to stitch the Working with a Pattern project choose a plain, medium-weight, cream cotton (allow sufficient fabric to fit your frame) and select a transfer method from the transfer section. The threads required are listed in the key: use three strands of Anchor Stranded Cotton, one strand of Anchor Pearl Cotton or two strands of Marlitt when stitching. On completion mount the work and frame it.

KEY

THREAD

ANCHOR STRANDED COTTON

1 Beige 362

2 Gold 307

3 Bronze 308

4 Beige 362, Gold 307 and Bronze 308 (one strand of each in the needle)

ANCHOR PEARL COTTON NO. 5

5 Medium Blue 131

ANCHOR MARLITT THREAD

6 Light Blue 1009

STITCHES

A Satin Stitch

B Blanket Stitch

C Backstitch

D Chain Stitch

E Stem Stitch

F Knotted Straight Stitch

G Trellis Filling Stitch

Thread Type
The type of thread required is shown above each set of numbers.

Thread Thickness
Anchor Pearl Cotton is available in three different thicknesses. The thickness is indicated by a number (in this case No.5).

Colour Mixtures
Occasionally the sewing thread is made up of a mixture of different colours. For example 4F indicates that one strand each of beige, bronze and gold Anchor Stranded Cottons were combined for the Knotted Straight Stitch.

Thread Mixtures
Some stitches are formed using different thread types and colours. For example, here, 2+5G – 2 for Anchor Stranded Cotton in gold and 5 for Anchor Pearl Cotton in medium blue.

Compound Stitches
When a stitch is made up of two colours the stitching directions are found in the stitch instructions. For example, for working G Trellis Filling Stitch, see page 89.

How Many Strands?
The number of strands required when stitching is found in the written instructions for each project.

The Thread
The number gives the type of thread, the colour and the colour code. For example, 2 indicates the thread is Anchor Stranded Cotton, the colour is gold and the colour code is 307.

The Stitch
The letter indicates the stitch to be used. For example, the letter C stands for backstitch.

The Dotted Line
The fine dotted line indicates the direction of the stitches.

WORKING FROM A CHART

A transfer is not required for projects using Aida. Aida is an evenweave fabric with easy-to-count threads which is ideal when stitches need to be the same size and evenly spaced. Designs worked on Aida come with an illustrated guide which shows the individual stitches plus a colour and stitch key. The thread colour is indicated by a number and the stitch by a letter. Work straight onto your fabric from the guide. You will find stitching is easier if you use a tapestry needle as a crewel needle can split the threads.

PROJECT INSTRUCTIONS

If you wish to stitch the Working from a Chart project choose 14-count cream Aida (allow sufficient fabric to fit your frame). The stitch instructions can be found in the Borders & Bands and Stems & Outlines chapters. The threads required are listed in the key: use one strand of Anchor Pearl Cotton and two strands of Marlitt when stitching.
On completion mount the work and frame it.

KEY

THREAD

ANCHOR PEARL COTTON NO. 5
1 Light Brown 365
2 Medium Blue 131

ANCHOR MARLITT THREAD
3 Light Blue 1009

STITCHES
A Holbein Stitch
B Blanket Stitch
C Feather Stitch
D Chevron Stitch
E Chinese Stitch
F Whipped
Running Stitch

STITCH NOTES
The thread colour is
indicated by a number
and the stitch by a letter.

Colour Mixtures
Some stitches are
formed using
different colours.
For example,
1+2A – 1 stands
for Anchor Pearl
Cotton in light
brown and 2 for
Anchor Pearl
Cotton in medium
blue.

Compound Stitches
When a stitch is
made up of two
colours the stitching
directions are found
in the stitch
instructions. For
example for
working A Holbein
Stitch, see page 45.

**How Many
Strands?**
The number of
strands required
when stitching is
found in the
written
instructions for
each project.

The Thread
The number gives the
type of thread, the
thickness, the colour and
the colour code. For
example 2 indicates the
thread is Anchor Pearl
Cotton No 5, the colour
is medium blue and the
colour code is 131.

The Stitch
The letter indicates
the stitch to be used.
For example, the
letter E stands for
Chinese stitch.

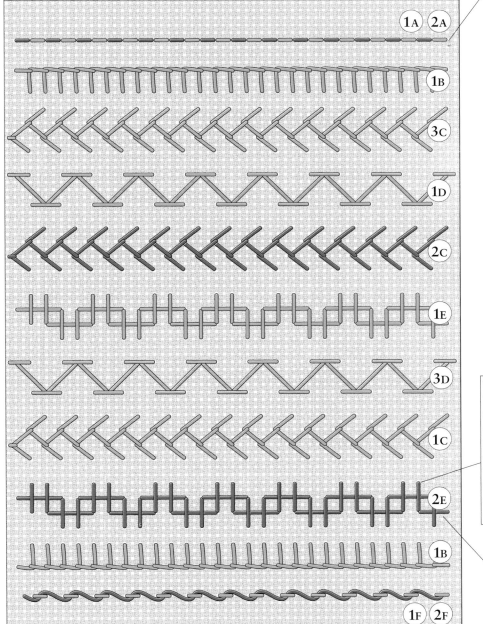

1A 2A
1B
3C
1D
2C
1E
3D
1C
2E
1B
1F 2F

EMBROIDERY HOOPS & FRAMES

Embroidery should always be worked in a hoop or a frame as this helps to reduce puckering. Fabric puckers when stitching is uneven and pulled too tightly. It is difficult to correct and can spoil the look of the embroidery when mounted, as illustrated below. There is a wide variety of hoops and frames available and choosing one can be puzzling, so I suggest you read the verdict boxes before buying one. It is not as difficult as it appears at first sight: frames can be classified according to their shape – either circular or rectangular.

*The benefit of working with a frame (right) can be clearly seen.
The embroidery on the left was worked without a frame
and now has puckers which cannot be removed.*

CIRCULAR HOOPS

A circular hoop (also known as a tambour frame) is made up of two rings with a tension screw on the outer hoop. The fabric is sandwiched between the outer and inner rings and secured by tightening the tension screw. Plastic flexi-hoops and spring hoops work on a similar principle but do not have the tension screw as the fabric is held firmly by the pressure of the outer ring which snaps very tightly over the rigid inner hoop.

Tambour frames and flexi-hoops are available in a wide range of sizes and the latter is also available in an oval shape.

RECTANGULAR FRAMES

Rectangular frames also divide into two main groups – roller or slate frames and artists' or embroidery stretchers – available in a range of sizes. A roller frame consists of four sections which assemble to form a rectangle with a roller at the top and bottom. The work is mounted in the frame by stitching it to the canvas webbing on the rollers and by lacing the sides. Unlike a roller frame, an artists' stretcher consists of a solid frame which cannot be adjusted once assembled. Fabric is attached to the wooden sides with drawing pins or staples.

Using a Circular Hoop

1 *Binding the hoop* Covering the inner hoop with tape such as bias binding helps to hold the fabric more securely in the frame and avoids marking. Tape the end of the binding at a 45° angle and wrap it around the hoop. Make sure the binding is tight and that there are no gaps. Pin the binding in position, cut off surplus tape, then stitch the end to secure it. Remove the pin.

2 *Preparing the fabric for the hoop* Before cutting your fabric to size it is important to check that you have allowed sufficient for mounting your work in a frame (see Fabric Allowance, page 9). Fabric edges can either be oversewn or pinked to stop fraying. Finally remove any creases in the fabric by lightly pressing with a steam iron.

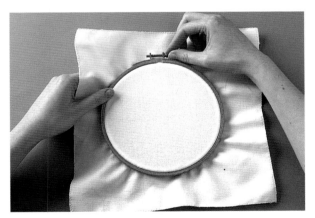

3 *Placing the fabric in the hoop* Place the bound inner hoop on a firm surface and lay the fabric right-side up over the top. Put the outer ring of the hoop over the top of the inner ring and the fabric to form a sandwich with the material in the centre. The tension screw on the outer ring should be at the top. Remove any slack by gently pulling the sides of the fabric. When the fabric is taut tighten the tension screw.

VERDICT

CIRCULAR HOOPS

✔ Hoops are inexpensive.

✔ They are available in a wide variety of sizes.

✔ They are light, easy to hold and easy to use.

✔ Flexi-hoops can be used as a decorative frame for work.

✗ The outer hoop can mark and stretch material; remove from the frame when not stitching.

✗ The material can become loose with stitching; adjust slack material from time to time.

Circular hoops are excellent for a beginner being cheap, easy to mount, adjust and use. Always select a frame which is larger than the design you intend to stitch.

Using a Roller Frame

1 *Preparing the fabric* Before cutting the fabric check that the width and length of fabric will fit the frame. The fabric should not be wider than the webbing on the roller and it should be long enough to reach the webbing on the opposite roller. The fabric's edges can either be oversewn or pinked to stop fraying. Remove any creases in the fabric by pressing with a steam iron.

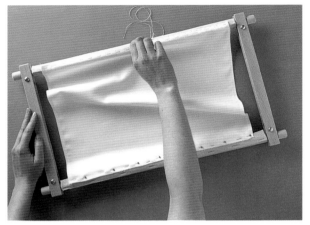

2 *Attaching the fabric* Pin one side of the fabric to the webbing on the top roller. Using a strong thread in a sharp-pointed needle, tack it to the edge of the webbing. When the tacking has been completed remove all the pins. Secure the edge of the fabric to the webbing by oversewing. Attach the lower part of the fabric to the bottom roller by repeating the same sequence.

3 *Lacing the sides* When the fabric has been attached to the webbing take up any slack material by turning the rollers. Centre the design in the middle of the frame. Now lace the sides of the fabric to the arms of the frame by taking the thread over, round and under the arms of the frame between each stitch. The fabric should be taut in the frame once both sides are laced.

VERDICT

ROLLER FRAMES

✓ Roller frames hold the fabric securely.

✓ They are suitable for larger projects.

✓ Work can remain in the frame until it is finished.

✓ Frames are available in a range of different sizes.

✗ They are not as easy to hold and use as a circular hoop.

✗ It takes time to mount the fabric.

A roller frame is excellent for larger projects and for work that needs to be held securely, but it is not as easy to use as a hoop for small projects.

Using a Stretcher Frame

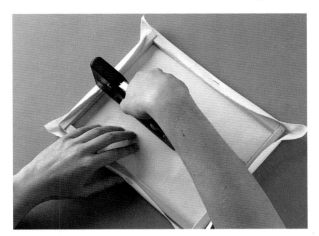

1 *Preparing the fabric* Before cutting the fabric check that it will fit the frame. The fabric can be attached to the frame with drawing pins or staples. If you are working with two layers of fabric – the embroidery fabric and backing – attach the backing to the frame first. Secure the backing with one staple in the centre of each side of the stretcher, ensuring the fabric is taut.

2 *Attaching the backing fabric* If the fabric is not as tight as you would like, remove one or two of the staples or drawing pins and pull the material tighter, then reattach them as before. Staple or pin along the top of the frame and then pull the fabric tight and repeat along the bottom edge. Now repeat to finish attaching the sides of the fabric to the sides of the stretcher frame.

3 *Attaching the surface fabric* Attach the fabric for embroidery over the backing by repeating the process, positioning the staples or drawing pins in the gaps between the staples or drawing pins which secure the backing. Artists' stretchers provide a wider and stronger frame for mounting fabric than the thinner embroidery frames, and are better suited for larger projects.

VERDICT

STRETCHER FRAMES

✓ Stretchers hold the fabric securely.

✓ They are easy to hold and to use.

✓ Work can stay in the frame until finished.

✓ Stretchers are available in different sizes.

✗ Embroidery stretchers are not very sturdy.

✗ It takes time to mount the fabric in the frame.

✗ The edges of the fabric can be damaged by pins or staples.

Embroidery stretchers are good for small to medium-size projects and artists' stretchers are excellent for large projects where the work needs to be held securely in a frame. This frame is not recommended for a beginner.

STARTING & FINISHING

How you start and finish your threads in embroidery is very important, as visible knots or bumps or loose threads can ruin the look of an otherwise perfectly worked embroidery. If you have trouble threading your needle with a speciality thread, such as gold thread, run the end through a block of beeswax before cutting and squeeze the fibres together.

Threading a Needle by Hand

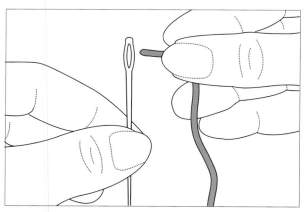

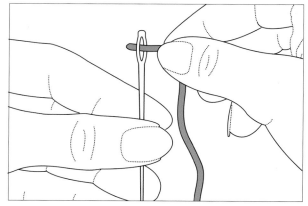

1 ***Selecting a needle*** Choose a needle with an eye large enough to take the thread but which is not too thick to pass easily through the fabric. Hold the needle between the thumb and finger of one hand with the end of the thread in the other.

2 ***Passing the thread through*** Check the end of the thread is not split as this will make threading difficult. Place the end of the thread at the eye and pass it through. Take hold of the end at the other side and pull it through.

Using a Needle Threader

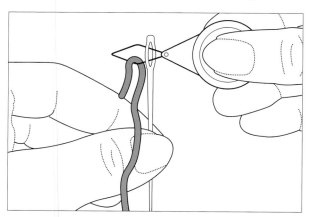

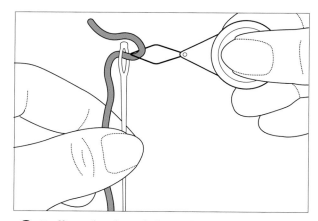

1 ***Passing the threader through*** Choose a needle with an eye large enough to take the thread but not too thick to pass easily through the fabric. Feed the wire loop through the eye of the needle and place the thread through the loop.

2 ***Pulling the thread through*** Pull the needle threader and thread back through the needle. This should be done gently as the wire loop on a needle threader is delicate and breaks easily. Your needle is threaded and ready for use.

Starting to Stitch

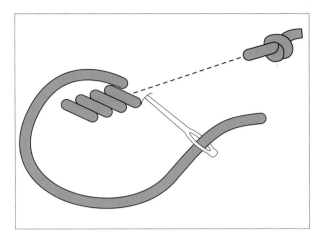

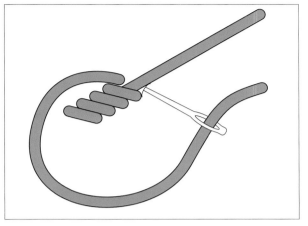

Starting with a knot Take the end of the thread, loop it round and bring the end through, pulling it tight to form the knot. The knot should be large enough to stop the end of the thread slipping through the fabric. Bring the needle through the material so that the knot lies neatly on the wrong side.

Starting without a knot Bring the needle and thread through to the right side of the fabric, leaving 5cm (2in) of thread at the back. Hold the end of the thread in position and take your embroidery stitches over the thread on the wrong side of the fabric. Three or four stitches will secure the end.

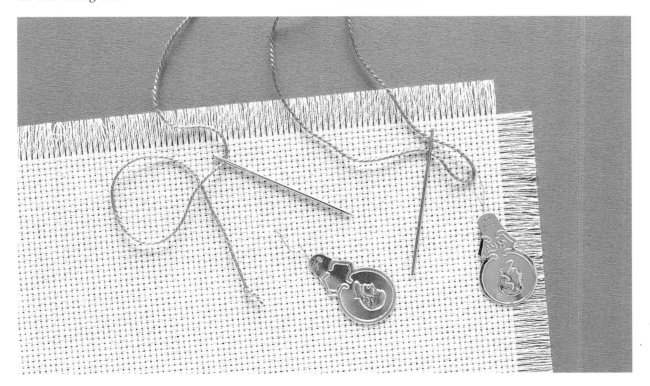

You will find threading a needle is easy if you select a needle with an eye large enough to take the thickness of thread. You may also find a needle threader useful.

Joining Threads

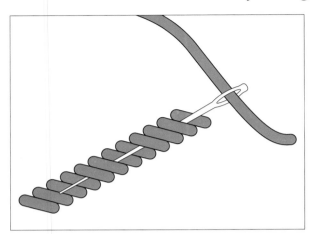

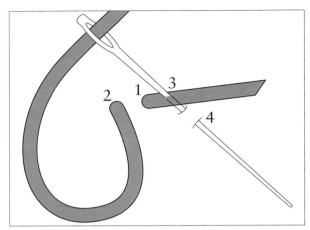

Method one Starting with the wrong side up, weave the needle and new thread through the back of the last few stitches. Pull the needle gently through to the right side of the fabric in the starting position, leaving a short tail on the back. Clip off this tail after a few stitches have secured the thread.

Method two Starting on the wrong side of the fabric, take a small stitch, as shown, and draw the thread through, leaving a short tail. Stitch through the end of the thread and bring the needle to the right side. Only use this method when it will be covered by a solid filling stitch such as satin stitch or split filling stitch.

Finishing Off

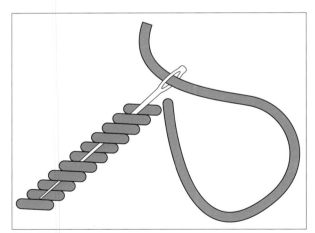

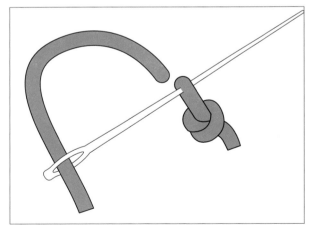

Finishing standard embroidery stitches Take the needle and thread through to the back of the work and weave the needle back through the underside of the last few stitches. Gently but firmly pull the needle and thread through and snip off the end of the thread to finish.

Finishing a French knot Take the needle and thread to the back of the work and stitch through the thread just above the knot. Take the needle back under the stitch and pass the needle through with the thread looped under the needle. Pull through and snip off the thread end.

MOUNTING WORK

*Many of the embroideries in this book can be displayed by mounting them in a frame.
A frame with glass in it not only enables you to show off the finished piece, but it protects it too,
keeping it clean of dust and away from grubby fingers. Either mount the picture straight in the
frame by lacing it to acid-free board or card or make and add a covered picture mount to go
round it. This is particularly useful if you wish to display a round or oval
embroidery in a square or rectangular frame.*

Lacing Your Work

1 *Preparing the card* Cut a piece of polyester wadding and thick card to fit the frame. Spread glue lightly over the card with a solid glue stick, then press the wadding onto the card. The wadding provides padding for the mounted work. If the project does not require any padding start at step two.

2 *Centring the card* Lay the embroidery face down on a clean, dry surface. Place the card padded-side down over the back of the work, using the tacking stitches to centre the card. (For details on how to prepare your fabric with tacking for mounting see Preparing Your Fabric, page 11).

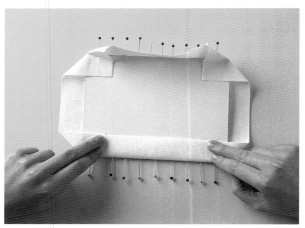

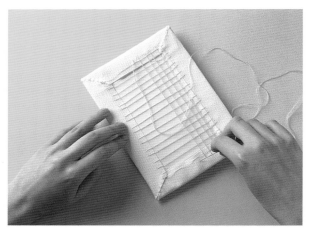

3 *Preparing the fabric edges* Hold the fabric in position by carefully pinning it to the sides of the mounting card. Fold the corners over onto the card diagonally, as shown, and secure with glue or masking tape. When all four corners have been firmly secured in this way, fold the fabric over, ready for lacing.

4 *Lacing the work* Fold the long edges of the fabric to the back and lace them together with strong thread in a large needle. Remove the pins on these edges. Repeat to lace the remaining edges together. The thread should be taut. Oversew the mitred corners then mount the card in the frame.

Covering a Mount with Fabric

1 *Attaching the fabric* Cut the fabric 2cm (³⁄₄in) larger all round than the mount. Spray the right side of the mount with repositionable spray glue. Do not apply too much – only a light covering is required. Lay the fabric right side down and place the glued mount face down in the centre.

2 *Mitring the corners* Turn the mount over and smooth out any air bubbles, then turn the mount over again to the back. Mitre each corner by folding over a flap and secure it with masking tape or glue. If you use glue, choose a solid glue stick as liquid glue may run or seep through and spoil the fabric.

3 *Neatening the edges* Run a line of glue along the edge of the mount with a solid glue stick. Turn each side edge over and press it firmly onto the glued surface to secure it. Add masking tape for extra security. Cut the centre of the fabric to within 2cm (³⁄₄in) of the mount as shown and snip into the fabric edges at 12mm (¹⁄₂in) intervals.

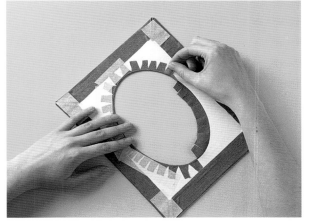

4 *Finishing the mount* Run a line of glue around the inner edge and fold back the tabs, one by one, pressing them firmly onto the glue. If you are making a large mount secure the tabs with masking tape as well for added strength. The mount is now ready for assembling in your chosen frame.

Framing Work in a Flexi-hoop

1 *Trapping the fabric* A flexi-hoop consists of two interlocking hoops, like an embroidery frame but without the tension screw. First remove the outer hoop by gently pulling it off. Place your fabric over the inner hoop, making sure that the design is centred. Firmly press the outer hoop back over the inner hoop, trapping the fabric between the rings.

2 *Trimming surplus material* If you intend to use your flexi-hoop as an embroidery frame, trim off the surplus fabric with a pair of sharp scissors, leaving a border of about 12mm (¹/₂in) around the edges. If you are working the stitches in an embroidery frame or hoop do not trim off excess fabric until you come to mount it in your flexi-hoop.

3 *Gathering the edges* Using a sharp needle and strong thread, run a line of small running stitches 6mm (¹/₄in) from the edge of the fabric, all the way round. Pull the thread so the fabric is gathered and drawn in at the back of the frame and knot it. If you are using a large flexi-hoop run a second line of running stitches around the opening for added security.

4 *Finishing the back* Cut out a felt circle 12mm (¹/₂in) smaller than the flexi-hoop. White felt is best – avoid using dark-coloured felts when using light-coloured surface fabrics as these may show through. Pin the felt securely over the opening at the back, covering the raw edges of the embroidery fabric. Slipstitch or oversew around the edge in matching sewing cotton to finish.

CHAPTER TWO

JUST FIVE STITCHES

*T*he projects in this chapter have been especially created for beginners
and those new to surface embroidery. Among the delightful beginner's
projects is an attractive bookmark and a set of colourful cards which are fun
to stitch. As you grow in confidence you will find that the eye-catching
Up & Away balloon picture (page 42) is easy to stitch.

One stitch has been chosen from each of the five stitch families to
form a basic set of stitches that will appear in all the chapters. These stitches,
which can be used to embroider just about anything, are backstitch,
French knot, lazy-daisy stitch, satin stitch and blanket stitch.

Backstitch

*This very useful stitch is from the stem and outline family and is used mainly to outline
objects and form stems, as on the Flower Vase Cards (page 39). It is one of the easiest
of the outline stitches and can be used for both straight and curved lines.*

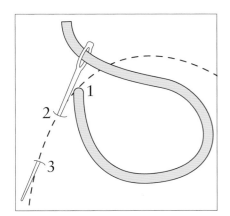

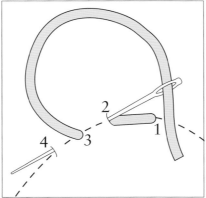

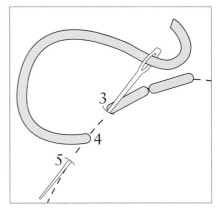

Bring the needle up at **1** and pull
the thread through. Go down at **2**,
then bring the needle up at **3** and
pull the thread through the fabric.

Insert the needle at **2** and bring it
up at **4**. Pull it through to form
the backstitch. Do not pull too
tightly as this can cause puckering.

Insert the needle at **3** and then
bring it up at **5**, as shown, to form
the next stitch. A backstitch line is
formed by repeating this sequence.

French Knot

This decorative knot is from the knot and dot family and is useful for forming the centre of flowers as shown in Practice Sampler No. 1 (page 34). French knots can be stitched either separately or in clusters to create a textured, three-dimensional effect.

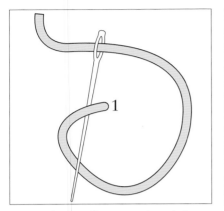
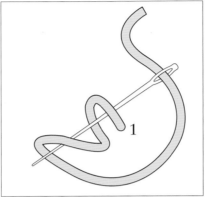
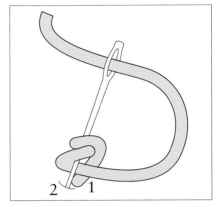

Bring the needle up at **1** and draw the thread through the fabric. Wind the thread around the needle by taking the thread over and under the needle.

Take the thread back over and under the needle for a second time. Pull the thread gently so that it tightens around the needle (but not too tightly).

Hold the thread to stop the stitch unravelling on the needle and insert the needle at **2**, close to **1**. Pull the thread through the fabric to form the knot.

Lazy-daisy Stitch

This pretty stitch is from the chain and loop family and is easy and quick to work. The lazy-daisy stitch, which consists of a single loop, is aptly named as it looks exactly like a flower petal and is consequently a very useful stitch for floral designs.

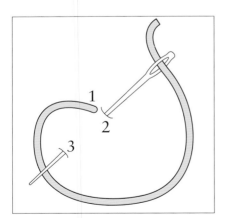
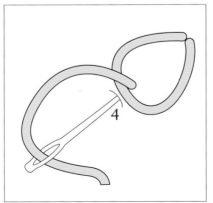
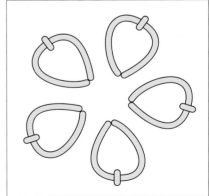

Bring the needle through at **1**. Insert the needle at **2** and bring it back up at **3**, making sure the thread runs underneath the needle, as shown.

Draw the needle through, take it over the looped thread and insert it at **4**, as shown. When the needle is drawn through at the back the loop is secured.

A lazy-daisy stitch can be worked either as a single stitch or in a small cluster radiating from a central point to suggest a pretty daisy flower.

Satin Stitch

This elegant stitch is from the solid and open filling stitch family and is extremely versatile – it can be used to fill almost any shape. Satin stitch is usually worked as a set of parallel lines, but the stitches can be easily fanned, making it a useful stitch for flower petals.

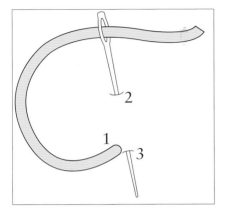 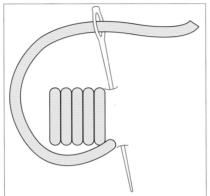 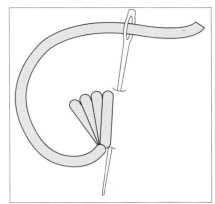

Bring the needle up at **1** and pull the thread through. Go down at **2** and bring the needle back out at **3**, next to **1**. Pull the thread through to form the first stitch.

Repeat the first sequence to create a set of parallel stitches. The tension is very important with this stitch – if the stitches are pulled too tightly puckering can occur.

Satin stitch can also be angled to produce a fan shape. This is formed by bringing the needle through the same hole at the base of the fan, as shown.

Blanket Stitch

This stitch is from the borders and bands family and can be used in a variety of ways. It can be worked with even spaces between the stitches or close together to form a broad filled band and it can be stitched both on a straight and a curved line.

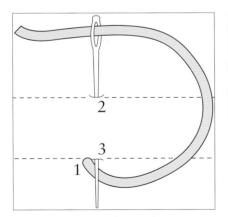 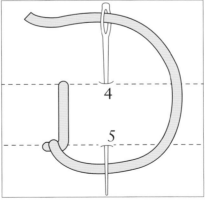 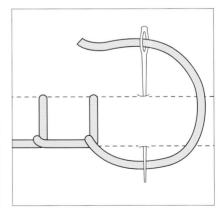

Create one straight stitch to start the line neatly by bringing the needle up at **1**. Go down at **2** and come up at **3** (which is immediately to the side of **1**).

Leave the required space and take the needle down at **4** and up at **5**, with the thread running behind the needle. Draw the needle through the fabric to form the stitch.

The blanket stitch pattern is formed by repeating this sequence. Try not to pull too tightly when drawing the thread through as this may cause puckering.

PROJECT ONE

PRACTICE SAMPLER NO. 1

*C*reate this pretty sampler and try out the five basic stitches in this chapter at the same time – backstitch, French knot, lazy-daisy stitch, satin stitch and blanket stitch. The sampler is worked on rich red fabric, but if you prefer to use a different colour you can easily change the thread colours to fit in with your choice.

YOU WILL NEED

At least 15cm (6in) square of medium-weight
*   red cotton sufficient to fit your frame*
Anchor Stranded Cotton in white 01, yellow 298
*   and green 243*
Yellow bow
Milward crewel needle No. 6 and sharp or
*   between sewing needle*
10cm (4in) flexi-hoop
10cm (4in) square of felt to finish the back
*   of the frame*
Sylko cotton thread in yellow and red

CREATIVE OPTIONS

The bouquet of daisies at the centre of this design would make an attractive card. Try stitching it on red felt and mounting it in a yellow or green card with a 6.5cm (2½in) circular aperture.

KEY

THREAD

ANCHOR STRANDED COTTON

1 White 01
2 Yellow 298
3 Green 243

STITCHES

A Backstitch
B French Knot
C Lazy-daisy Stitch
D Satin Stitch
E Blanket Stitch

STITCH NOTES

The thread colour is indicated by a number and the stitch by a letter.

1 Transfer the design to the fabric using a method suitable for coloured fabric such as dressmakers' carbon (see pages 11-15). Mount the prepared fabric in a frame – you can either use an embroidery hoop or mount the fabric in your flexi-hoop (see pages 20-23).

2 Start the embroidery in the centre and use three strands of Anchor Stranded Cotton in a crewel needle. When the embroidery is finished attach the bow to the centre of the bouquet, as shown in the picture, left. Secure it with a few stitches of yellow cotton using your sharp or between needle.

3 On completion remove the embroidery from the frame and lightly press it on the wrong side with a steam iron, if required, to remove any slight puckering.

4 If you have stitched the design in an embroidery hoop, trim off the excess fabric and mount the work in your flexi-hoop. If you have stitched the design in your flexi-hoop, trim the excess fabric to within 12mm (½in) of the frame. Gather in the fabric at the back and cover with felt (see page 30).

THREAD AND FABRIC OPTIONS

• The sampler would look equally pretty stitched in Anchor Pearl Cotton No. 5. This is thicker than Anchor Stranded Cotton so you will only need one length of thread in the needle.

• If you wish to use a light-weight fabric instead of the medium-weight one used here, reinforce the back with iron-on interfacing – lay a 15cm (6in) square of interfacing on the back of the fabric and lightly iron with a steam iron.

PROJECT TWO

FUCHSIA BOOKMARK

*C*reate this eye-catching bookmark for yourself or as a present for someone
special using backstitch, satin stitch, blanket stitch and lazy-daisy stitch.
This beautiful cascade of fuchsias would also make a delightful cake band –
simply repeat the pattern until the band reaches the desired length.
The finished bookmark is 25.5 x 5cm (10 x 2in).

YOU WILL NEED

*At least 25.5 x 12.5cm (10 x 5in) of white
    evenweave fabric sufficient to fit your frame*
*20.5 x 12.5cm (8 x 5in) rectangle of light-weight
    iron-on interfacing*
*Anchor Stranded Cotton in pale pink 6, light pink
    8, medium pink 38, deep pink 39, golden
    yellow 307 and medium green 226*
*Milward crewel needle No. 6 and a sharp or
    between sewing needle*
Sylko cotton thread in white

1 Transfer the design to the fabric – use a
soluble pen, transfer pencil or dressmakers'
carbon (see pages 11-15).

2 Place the iron-on interfacing face
down on the back of the fabric, making
sure it is centred over the design and is in
line with the weave of the fabric. Fuse the
interfacing to the fabric by lightly pressing
with a steam iron.

THREAD OPTIONS

You can add a touch of sparkle to your bookmark
by stitching the flowers with Anchor Marlitt rayon
thread. Marlitt thread has four strands. As it is
thicker than Anchor Stranded Cotton you will only
need two strands for stitching.

HANDY HINTS

Before attaching the interfacing draw out one thread
near the top of the fabric which will mark the line for
the row of blanket stitches. You must allow at least
2.5cm (1in) above this line for the fringe. You can also
use the drawn thread to help you align the interfacing
with the fabric weave.

KEY

THREAD

ANCHOR STRANDED COTTON

1 Pale Pink 6
2 Light Pink 8
3 Medium Pink 38
4 Deep Pink 39
5 Golden Yellow 307
6 Medium Green 226

STITCHES

A Backstitch
B Satin Stitch
C Blanket Stitch
D Lazy-daisy Stitch

STITCH NOTES

The thread colour is indicated by a number and the stitch by a letter. The fine dotted lines indicate the direction of the stitch.

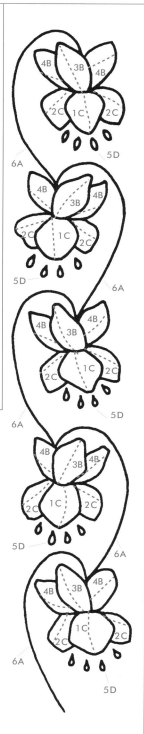

3 Mount the prepared fabric in a frame large enough to see the complete design (see pages 20-23) – an embroidery hoop should be sufficient.

4 Using three strands of Anchor Stranded Cotton in a crewel needle, start the embroidery at the top of the bookmark and complete each flower before starting the next.

5 When all the flowers have been worked, run a line of blanket stitches across the top and bottom of the bookmark approximately 12mm (¹⁄₂in) from the design. Check the weave of the fabric to make sure the stitching is straight.

6 Remove the work from the frame and trim the fabric so it is 12.5cm (5in) wide with the embroidery centred and with a border of 2.5cm (1in) at the top and bottom for the fringes.

7 Fringe the top and bottom edges by prising out the horizontal threads with your fingers or a needle. Fold over the fabric on each side of the embroidery so that the bookmark is 5cm (2in) wide and lightly press the folds with a steam iron.

8 Turn the bookmark over, fold the top flap under to form a 6mm (¹⁄₄in) hem and slipstitch it the length of the bookmark using white sewing cotton in a sewing needle. Finally, trim the ends of the fringes to straighten them, if necessary.

CREATIVE OPTIONS

You could use this design to make an attractive trimming for bed linen by running the repeat pattern down the side of pillowcases and along the top edge of a sheet or duvet cover.

FLOWER VASE CARDS

*T*hese cheering cards feature beautiful vases worked in satin stitch
and backstitch. Out of them spill flowers, stems and leaves in lazy-
daisy stitch, blanket stitch and French knots. They are worked on brightly
coloured pieces of felt, although you could use a different base
fabric or choose softer colours if you wish.

YOU WILL NEED

*At least 10cm (4in) square of felt sufficient
to fit your frame*

*10cm (4in) square of light-weight iron-on
interfacing*

*Anchor Stranded Cottons as given in the
chart for each vase*

Milward crewel needle No. 6

Card with an 8cm (3¼in) circular aperture

Solid glue stick

HANDY HINTS

If you intend to mount your work in dark-coloured
cards, as shown, stick a square of white paper in
the mounting flap before attaching your embroidery.
This will stop the dark background from showing
through the felt and making the colour less bright.

1 Lay out the fabric right-side down. Place the
interfacing glue-side down on the centre of the
fabric and lightly press with a steam iron to fuse
the layers together. Turn the fabric over.

2 Transfer the design to the fabric (see pages
11-15). A transfer pencil is best as care needs
to be taken not to damage the surface of the felt.
Make sure the design is centred on the felt.

3 Start the embroidery in the centre of the
design using three strands of Anchor Stranded
Cotton in a crewel needle.

4 Remove the finished embroidery from the
frame and trim so the fabric is 12mm (½in)
wider than the card's aperture. Apply an even
layer of glue from a glue stick on the mounting
flap (the area behind the aperture). Place the
fabric in position and lightly press to secure.

KEY

THREAD

ANCHOR STRANDED COTTON
1 Yellow 289
2 Orange 330
3 Red 46
4 Green 239
5 Blue 433

STITCHES
A Backstitch
B Satin Stitch
C French Knot
D Lazy-daisy Stitch
E Blanket Stitch

STITCH NOTES
The thread colour is indicated by a number and the stitch by a letter. The fine dotted lines indicate the direction of the stitch.

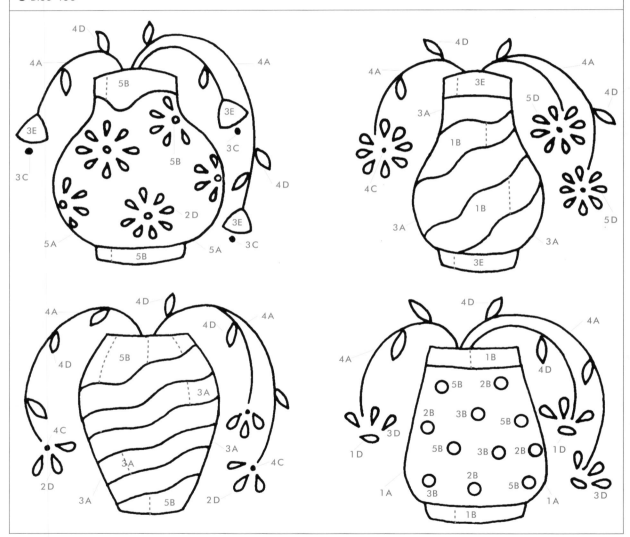

THREAD OPTIONS

These cards would look good stitched in many different threads from stranded cottons to soft wools. You can add a touch of sparkle by stitching with Anchor Marlitt thread or create subtle tones by using Bond Multis thread which has a splash of random colour.

UP & AWAY

This colourful balloon is worked in satin stitch with strings of backstitch, a basket of blanket stitch and ballast worked in pretty lazy-daisy stitch.

YOU WILL NEED

At least 28 x 23cm (11 x 9in) of blue medium-weight cotton sufficient to fit your frame

Anchor Stranded Cotton in light pink 9, medium pink 11, light lemon 300, medium lemon 301, light blue 144, medium blue 146, light green 254 and medium green 255

Milward crewel needle No. 6 and a sharp or between sewing needle

Frame with a 17.5 x 12.5cm (7 x 5in) aperture

Card mount to fit the frame with a 12.5 x 7.5cm (5 x 3in) aperture

Card for lacing to fit the frame

Drima extra-strong thread for lacing

1 Transfer the design onto the fabric using a soluble pen or transfer pencil (see pages 12-13). Mount the prepared fabric in frame – an embroidery hoop or flexi-frame is ideal (see pages 21 and 30).

2 Using three strands of Anchor Stranded Cotton in a crewel needle start the embroidery at the top of the balloon and gradually work down to the basket. Take care when satin stitching the balloon – if you pull the thread too tight the fabric will pucker.

3 On completion remove the embroidery from the frame and lightly press it on the wrong side with a steam iron. Trim and then lace the embroidery to the card (see page 28) and mount it in a frame.

FABRIC OPTIONS

Why not change the blue cotton base fabric for a blue synthetic fabric which adds a shine to the sky? If you choose light-weight fabric you will need a light-weight cotton as a backing. Mount the layers together in a frame and stitch through both at the same time.

KEY

THREAD
ANCHOR STRANDED COTTON
1 Light Pink 9
2 Medium Pink 11
3 Light Lemon 300
4 Medium Lemon 301
5 Light Blue 144
6 Medium Blue 146
7 Light Green 254
8 Medium Green 255

STITCHES
A Satin Stitch
B Blanket Stitch
C Backstitch
D Lazy-daisy Stitch

STITCH NOTES
The thread colour is indicated by a number and the stitch by a letter. The fine dotted lines indicate the direction of the stitch.

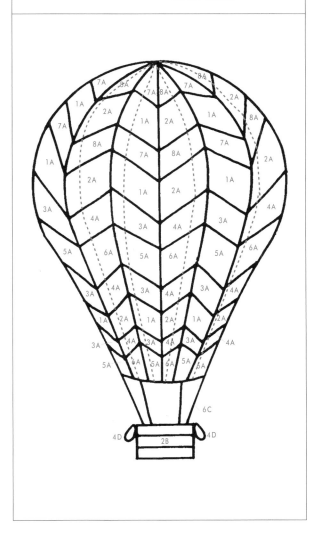

CHAPTER THREE

STEMS & OUTLINES

*T*he stitches in this family are used for working the outlines of shapes and for
adding fine details such as stems or ropes. All the projects in this chapter are
worked almost entirely from outline stitches. These are quick and easy to stitch and
therefore ideal for larger projects such as the Friendly Dragon Bag (page 55).

*The six stitches featured in the stems and outlines family are backstitch, couching, coral
stitch, Holbein stitch, stem stitch and whipped running stitch. You can learn these stitches
by working Practice Sampler No. 2 (page 48) and then extend your expertise by stitching
the High Fliers picture (page 50) which also contains the complete set of stitches.*

Backstitch

This useful stitch, which is also featured in the basic set of five stitches, is the easiest of the outline stitches and can be used for both straight and curved lines. For added decoration backstitch can be embellished with a second thread in another colour in the same way as whipped running stitch (page 47).

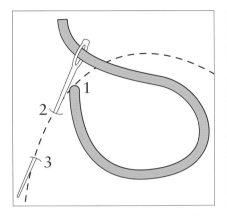
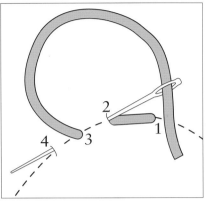
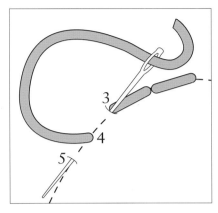

Bring the needle up at **1** and pull the thread through. Go down at **2**, then bring the needle up at **3** and pull the thread through the fabric.

Insert the needle at **2** and bring it up at **4**. Pull it through to form the backstitch. Do not pull too tightly as this can cause puckering.

Insert the needle at **3** and then bring it up at **5**, as shown, to form the next stitch. A backstitch line is formed by repeating this sequence.

Holbein Stitch

Also known as double running stitch, this simple stitch produces an identical line of stitching on both sides of the fabric, so it is often associated with blackwork. This stitch can either be worked in one colour or with contrasting threads, as shown.

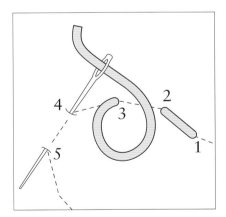
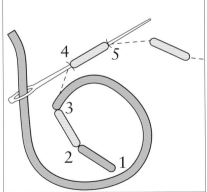
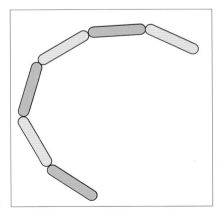

Lay down a line of evenly spaced running stitches as follows. Bring the needle up at **1**, go down at **2** and pull the needle out at **3**. Repeat the sequence by going down at **4** and coming up at **5**.

Work a second line of running stitches in reverse, bringing the needle up and out at **1**, going down at **2** and pulling the needle out at **3**. Repeat the sequence by going down at **4** and coming up at **5**.

The double lines of running stitch produce a solid, continuous line which can be stitched straight or on a curved line. It can also be decorated like whipped running stitch (see page 47).

Stem Stitch

This aptly named stitch is ideal for representing flower stalks. The stitches overlap to give added width and texture to the effect and they can be worked to produce a straight or curved line. Try to keep stitch lengths and overlapping positions even.

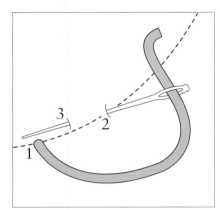

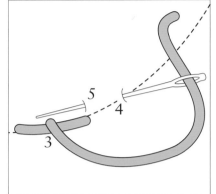

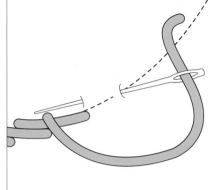

Bring the needle up and out at **1**. Insert the needle at **2** (which is slightly to the right-hand side of the line to be stitched) and come up and out at **3**.

Repeat the sequence by inserting the needle at **4** and coming up and out at **5** to form the next stitch. Do not pull too tightly as this can cause puckering.

For the best effect the stitches should be evenly spaced, the same length and overlap at the same point each time to give a line of consistent thickness.

Couching

This is the method of attaching thread to the fabric so that it lies on the surface and runs in a continuous line. It is done by using a second thread, which can be a matching or contrasting thread, to overlap and hold the surface thread securely. Couching can be worked on a straight or curved line.

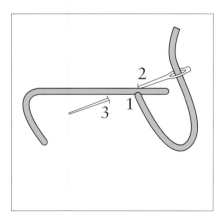

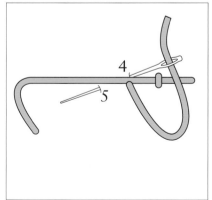

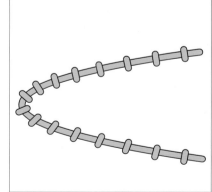

Bring the thread to be couched through the fabric and hold it in position while you secure it. Bring the couching thread up at **1**, insert it at **2** and then bring it up at **3**.

Take the needle over the thread again, insert it at **4** and come up at **5**. Repeat. Secure the couched thread at each end on the wrong side with a few stitches.

Couching stitches should be evenly spaced, especially when using a contrasting thread. When stitching with a matching thread, close up the spaces on sharp curves.

Whipped Running Stitch

This quick and simple decorative outline stitch is very versatile – it can be worked in small or large stitches and in straight or curved lines. It can also be stitched with dual colours using different types of thread to produce interesting textures.

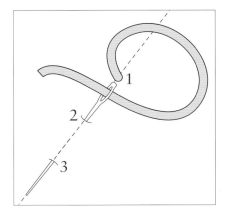

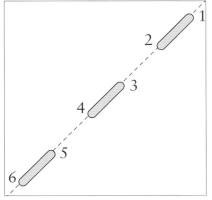

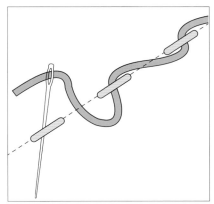

Work a line of running stitches – start by bringing the needle up and out at **1**; take the needle down at **2** and bring it up and out at **3**, as shown.

Complete the line by repeating the sequence from **2** to **3**. The stitches should be evenly spaced and large enough for a needle to pass underneath.

Lace a second thread through the running stitches by passing the needle under the stitch, as shown. Pull through and repeat under the next stitch.

Coral Stitch

This decorative stitch forms an attractive outline by attaching the thread to the fabric by a series of evenly spaced knots. It is useful for adding texture to line work and it can also be stitched in a straight or curved line.

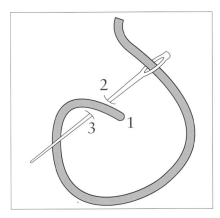

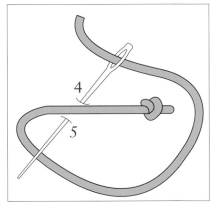

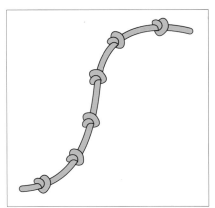

Bring the needle up and out at **1**. Lay the thread flat and insert the needle at **2**, bringing it up at **3** with the thread looped under the needle. Pull the thread through.

Lay the thread flat again and insert the needle at **4**, bringing it up and out at **5** with the thread looped under the needle. Make sure the knots are evenly spaced.

Repeat this sequence to form a line of coral stitches. To avoid slack thread between the stitches, hold the thread in place while pulling the needle through.

PRACTICE SAMPLER NO. 2

*A*ll the stitches in this chapter feature in this sampler – backstitch,
Holbein stitch, stem stitch, couching, coral and whipped running
stitch. By making it into a useful pin cushion you will have your sample stitches close
to hand. The stitches are worked on Aida evenweave fabric because it has easy-to-count
squares which simplifies stitching. There's no need to transfer the design
to the fabric – you can work straight from the chart.

YOU WILL NEED

*Two squares at least 18.5cm (7¼in) of 14-count
yellow Aida sufficient to fit your frame*
*Anchor Pearl Cotton No. 5 in orange 316 and
green 225*
*Milward tapestry, crewel and sharp or between
needles*
*Sylko cotton thread in yellow to sew the
seams of the pin cushion*
Wadding for filling

1 Mount the fabric in a frame (see pages 20-23).
Working straight from the chart, start in the
centre of the sampler with a square of backstitch,
working each stitch over two fabric squares with
four stitches to each side. Use one strand of Anchor
Pearl Cotton in a tapestry needle.

2 Leave a space of four rows between each line
of stitching. Use orange thread to couch the
next line over green thread, stitching into every
second square, as shown in the sample, right.

3 Stitch the coral stitch line by forming a knot
on every second square. You will find it easier
to work the knots with a crewel needle.

HANDY HINTS

Always use a tapestry needle when stitching on
evenweave fabric such as Aida – a tapestry needle
glides smoothly through the holes without splitting
the fabric threads.

4 Stitch the fourth line in Holbein stitch, using a tapestry needle and working each stitch over two squares.

5 Stem stitch the fifth line over two squares with a tapestry needle. Stem stitch will not flow around corners so work each side separately.

6 Stitch the outer line in whipped running stitch with a tapestry needle over two squares.

7 On completion remove the embroidery from the frame, trim to size and lightly press it on the wrong side with a steam iron. Pin the two squares together with right sides facing and machine a 12mm (½in) seam around the edge,

leaving a 7.5cm (3in) opening in one side. Clip the corners for ease and turn the work right sides out.

8 Press and then fill the cover with small pieces of wadding until the pad is firm. Turn in the raw edges at the opening and slipstitch the folds together to finish.

FABRIC OPTIONS

If you do not wish to use Aida fabric you could use a small checked fabric such as cotton gingham. If you use gingham, bond a square of medium-weight iron-on interfacing to the back of the fabric before stitching the design with a crewel needle.

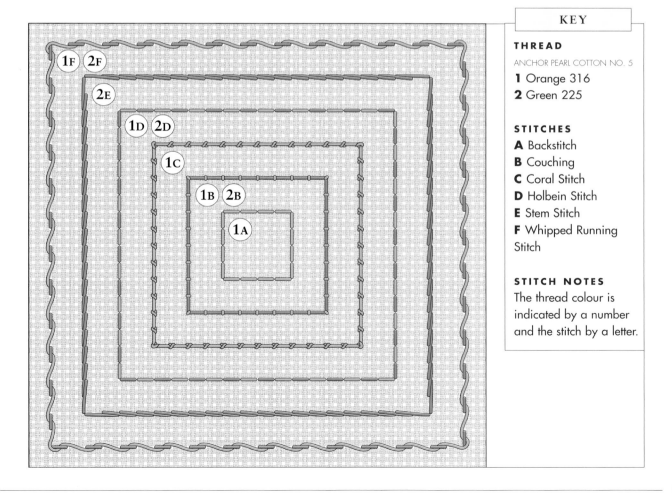

KEY

THREAD
ANCHOR PEARL COTTON NO. 5
1 Orange 316
2 Green 225

STITCHES
A Backstitch
B Couching
C Coral Stitch
D Holbein Stitch
E Stem Stitch
F Whipped Running Stitch

STITCH NOTES
The thread colour is indicated by a number and the stitch by a letter.

HIGH FLIERS

*T*his unusual kite picture features all six stem and outline stitches.
The dancing kites are embroidered with Anchor Stranded Cotton
in soft pastel tones but you could easily change the colour scheme and
produce an equally stunning picture in primary colours.

KEY

THREAD

ANCHOR STRANDED COTTON

1 Lemon 300
2 Green 259
3 Pink 6

STITCHES

A Backstitch
B Couching (couch
with Green thread
over Pink)
C Coral Stitch
D Holbein Stitch
E Stem Stitch
F Whipped Running
Stitch (Lemon
whipped in Pink)

STITCH NOTES

The thread colour is
indicated by a number
and the stitch by a letter.

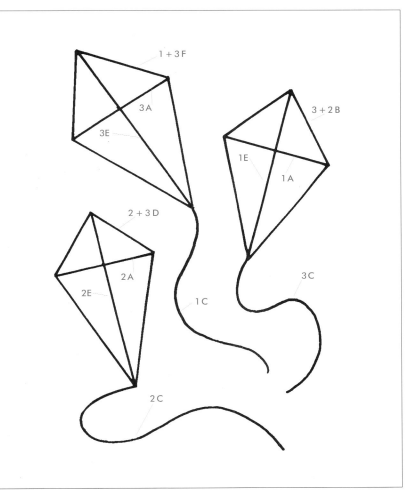

YOU WILL NEED

*At least 28 x 23cm (11 x 9in) of medium-weight
    blue cotton fabric sufficient to fit your frame*
*Anchor Stranded Cotton in lemon 300, green 259
    and pink 6*
Milward crewel needle with a large eye (No. 5)
*Frame with an internal aperture of 16.5 x 11.5cm
    (6$^{1}/_{2}$ x 4$^{1}/_{2}$in)*
Card for lacing to fit the frame
Drima extra-strong thread for lacing
*Card mount to fit the frame with an internal
    aperture 12 x 8cm (4$^{3}/_{4}$ x 3$^{1}/_{4}$in)*

1 Prepare the fabric by transferring the design to
the fabric – use a soluble pen, transfer pencil
or dressmakers' carbon (see pages 11-15). Mount
the prepared fabric in an embroidery hoop or
frame (see pages 20-23).

2 Work the stitches following the chart and
using all six strands of Anchor Stranded
Cotton – you will need a sharp, slender needle
with a large eye.

3 On completion remove the embroidery from
the frame and lightly press it on the wrong
side with a steam iron. Lace the work to the card
(see page 28) and then fit it in a frame behind
your card mount.

PROJECT THREE

GOLDEN DRAGONFLIES

....

*T*he delicate charm of dragonflies hovering above the water is captured in

this beautiful goldwork picture which uses just two stitches – satin stitch

(page 33) and couching. The design is worked on deep blue silk to give the feeling

of rippling water, so it requires a transfer method suitable for both a deep colour

and delicate fabric such as dressmakers' carbon or tacking.

YOU WILL NEED

*At least 28 x 23cm (11 x 9in) of deep-blue silk
sufficient to fit your frame*

*Light-weight cotton for backing the same size
as your silk*

*Anchor Stranded Cotton in blue 162 and
green 224*

*Kreinik Gold Thread in Japan gold No. 7, Japan
gold No. 5 and Japan gold No. 002J*

Milward fine, sharp-pointed needle for couching

Milward crewel needle with a large eye (No. 5)

*Milward sharp or between needle for lacing
the embroidery to the card*

*Frame with an internal aperture of 16.5 x 11.5cm
(6$^{1}/_{2}$ x 4$^{1}/_{2}$in)*

Card for lacing to fit the frame

Wadding the same size as the card

Solid glue stick

Drima extra-strong thread for lacing

1 Transfer the design onto the fabric (see pages 11-15). Mount the prepared fabric and backing together in a frame (see pages 20-23).

2 Use three strands of Anchor Stranded Cotton in a crewel needle to stitch the heads and bodies of the dragonflies. Outline the body and then the wings with the thickest gold thread (No. 7) and couch the line with one strand of fine gold thread in a fine, sharp-pointed needle. Stitch the legs and antennae using the same method. Use the medium-weight gold thread (No. 5) for the interior of the wings and couch with one strand of fine gold thread.

3 On completion remove the embroidery from the frame and lightly press it on the wrong side with a steam iron. Glue the wadding to the card and lace the work on top (see page 28). Fit the laced embroidery in the frame.

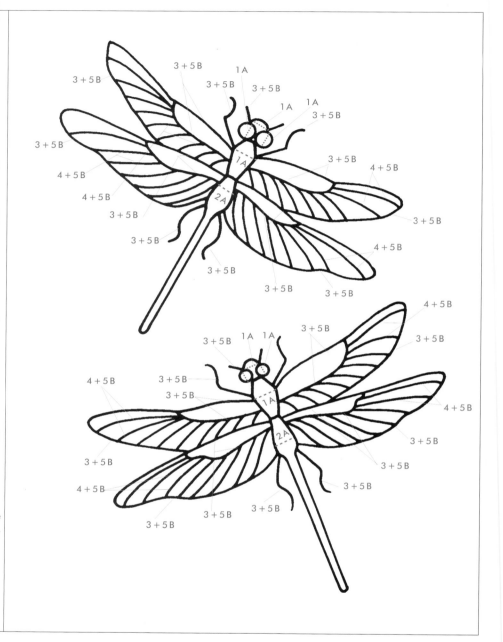

KEY

THREAD

ANCHOR STRANDED COTTON

1 Green 224
2 Blue 162

KREINIK GOLD THREAD

3 Japan Gold No. 7
4 Japan Gold No. 5
5 Japan Gold No. 002J

STITCHES

A Satin Stitch (page 33)
B Couching

STITCH NOTES

The thread colour is indicated by a number and the stitch by a letter. The fine dotted lines indicate the direction of the stitch.

GOLD THREADS

To avoid scuffing the gold thread for couching enlarge the hole at the points where the thread is brought to the surface at the beginning and end. This should be done carefully with a stiletto or thick needle – the hole should only be large enough for the thread to slip through comfortably.

HANDY HINTS

Speciality threads, like gold threads, are generally more delicate than stranded or pearl cottons, so treat them with particular care. Stitch with short lengths to reduce wear and slide the needle along the thread as you work. This prevents the needle rubbing against a particular point on the thread.

FRIENDLY DRAGON BAG

*S*titch this fun dragon bag for a child to use at school or at home for treasured toys. The dragon is worked in all six of this chapter's stitches plus its eyes and nostrils are worked in satin stitch (page 33) to give them greater emphasis. It is quick to work and the bag is simple to make.

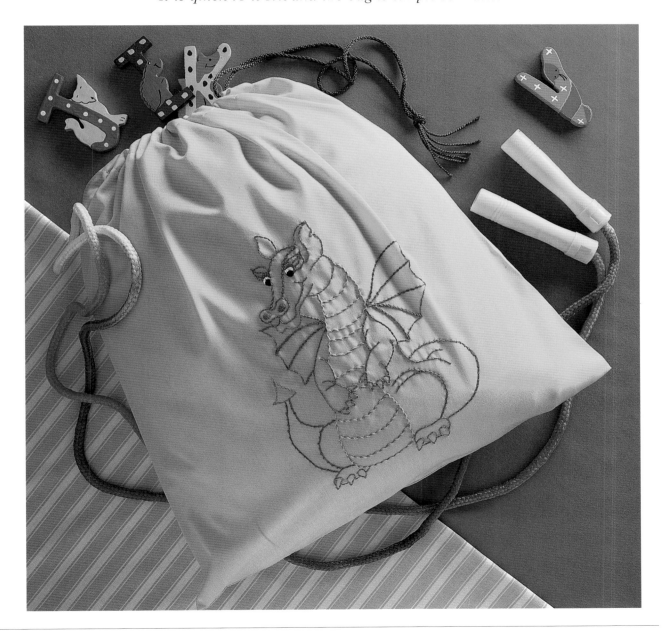

YOU WILL NEED

47 x 84cm (18½ x 33in) of medium-weight yellow cotton

Anchor Stranded Cotton in white 01, gold 307, brown 309, green 239 and navy blue 127

Milward crewel needle No. 6 and a sharp or between needle

50cm (½ yard) of green cord

Sylko cotton thread in a matching colour

1 Trace the design and go over the lines with a transfer pencil (see page 13). Fold the fabric in half so that the fold runs down one side of the bag. Centre the transfer over the folded material (make allowance for the side seam) and 7.5cm (3in) from the bottom of the fabric. Iron to transfer the design, then mount the fabric in a rectangular frame (see pages 22-23).

2 Beginning at the centre of the design, stitch all parts of the dragon with three strands of Anchor Stranded Cotton in a crewel needle, starting with the outlines and then going on to the details such as the eyes and claws. Threads should not be taken across the back in such a way that they show through the fabric on the right side. Instead, weave the needle along the back of the stitches to reach a new stitching position.

3 On completion remove the embroidery from the frame and lightly press it on the wrong side with a steam iron. Fold the fabric in half with right sides facing and machine a 12mm (½in) seam along the bottom and up the side to form the bag. Overlock or zigzag stitch the raw edges together to prevent fraying.

4 Turn over 12mm (½in) of fabric at the top and lightly press the fold. Turn the fabric again to form a 4cm (1½in) hem. Machine stitch the hem, leaving a 5cm (2in) opening at the seam for the cord to go through.

5 Insert the cord and knot the two strands 7.5cm (3in) from the ends. Allow the ends of the cord to unravel to form the tassel. Lightly press the tassel to remove the crinkles.

HANDY HINTS

Take care that all threads are securely fastened as the bag will need to be child proof. Also avoid thread loops on the back of the work as the contents of the bag could catch on them and spoil the embroidery.

COLOUR OPTIONS

You can easily change both the colour of the fabric and the threads for this project, choosing your child's favourite colours or opting for a bright or soft colour combination.

KEY

THREAD

ANCHOR STRANDED COTTON

1 White 01

2 Gold 307

3 Brown 309

4 Green 239

5 Navy Blue 127

STITCHES

A Backstitch

B Coral Stitch

C Couching

D Stem Stitch

E Holbein Stitch

F Whipped Running Stitch (Brown whipped in Gold)

G Satin Stitch (page 33)

STITCH NOTES

The thread colour is indicated by a number and the stitch by a letter. The fine dotted lines indicate the direction of the stitch.

CHAPTER FOUR

KNOTS & DOTS

*K*nots and dots are mainly used as filling stitches or for emphasising the smaller details in a design. They are invaluable for depicting the centre of flowers or small details such as eyes but they can also be used to create texture as in the Scarecrow & Friend picture (page 64). Knots and dots can also form the main stitches in an embroidery as in the striking Fireworks Display picture (page 66).

The six stitches featured in the knot and dot family are French knot, knotted straight stitch, Danish knot, four-legged knot, bullion knot and seeding. You can learn these stitches by working Practice Sampler No. 3 (page 62).

French Knot

This stitch creates a neat raised knot which is the most useful and versatile of all the knot stitches.
French knots can be stitched either separately or in clusters to create a textured surface.

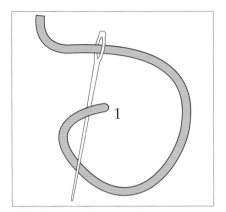 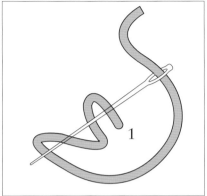 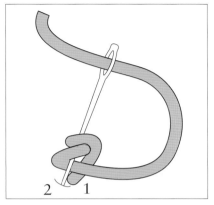

Bring the needle up at **1** and pull the thread through the fabric. Wind the thread around the needle by taking the thread over and under the needle.

Take the thread back over and under the needle for a second time. Pull the thread gently so that it tightens around the needle (but not too tightly).

Hold the thread to stop the stitch unravelling on the needle and insert the needle at **2**, close to **1**. Pull the thread through the fabric to form the knot.

Knotted Straight Stitch

This compound stitch is made from a straight stitch and a French knot. It is useful for
working the stamens in flowers such as poppies. It can also be used to form petals
as in the Practice and Medieval Strawberry Samplers (pages 62 and 69).

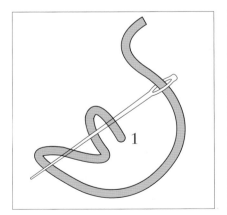 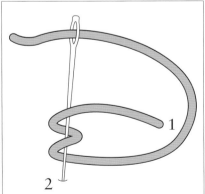 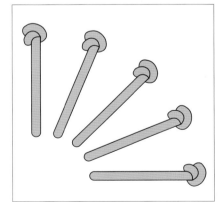

Bring the needle up and out at **1** and wind the thread twice round the needle by taking the thread up, over and down under the needle, then winding the thread round the needle a second time.

Pull the thread gently so that it tightens around the needle (but not too tightly). Hold the thread to stop the stitch unravelling on the needle, then insert it at **2**, as shown in the diagram.

Pull the needle and thread through to the back of the fabric to form one long stitch with a small, neat knot at the end. This stitch can be worked to form a set of parallel or fanned lines.

Danish Knot

A dense triangular-shaped knot is formed by this stitch which makes an interesting and highly decorative filling stitch. To increase the effect use a round, twisted thread such as pearl cotton.

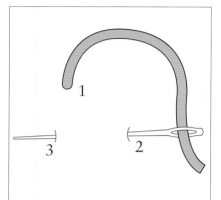

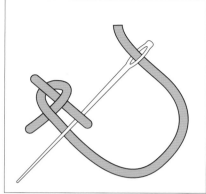

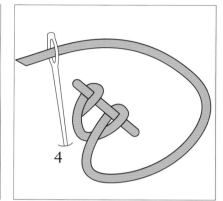

Bring the needle up at **1** and go down at **2** to form a short bar. Bring the needle up at **3**, halfway along the bar and to one side; draw the thread through.

Take the thread over the bar and pass the needle through to form a loop. Pass the needle under the bar again with the thread under the needle, as shown.

Draw the needle and thread through. Take the needle down at **4** and pull the thread to the back to form the knot. To add variation, work knots in different threads.

Bullion Knot

This tubular-shaped knot can be adjusted in length and thickness. When bullion knots are stitched in clusters they make an interesting textured filling stitch. However, they can also be used as an outline stitch – to form the petals of a flower, for example.

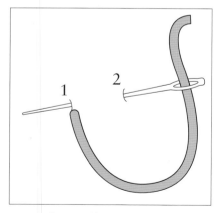

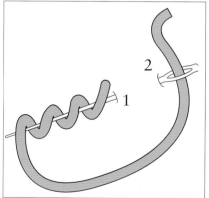

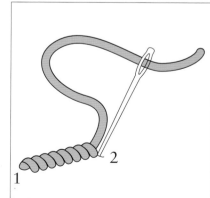

Bring the needle up and out at **1**. Take the needle down at **2** and bring it partway up at **1**, which is where you started. Leave the needle in this position, ready to form the knot.

Wind the thread around the needle – the number of times depends on how long and thick you want the knot to be. Rest your finger on the coil and pull the needle through.

Release the coil as you pull the needle and thread through. The knot will lie flat as you take the needle back to **2**. Take the needle down and through at **2**, as shown, to finish.

Four-legged Knot

These attractive knotted crosses make interesting and decorative filling stitches. They can be worked singly or in small groups to represent flowers. The texture of the stitch can be varied by stitching with different threads and the size of the stitch is easily adjusted.

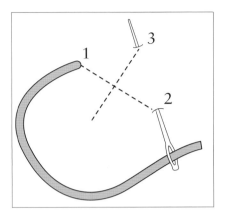

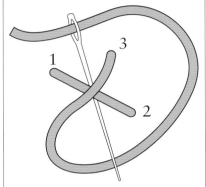

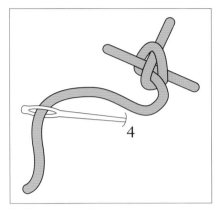

Take the needle up and draw the thread through at **1**. Take the needle down at **2** and bring it up in the centre and to the right at **3**; draw the thread through.

Pass the thread across the first stitch and then slip the needle under the bar. Loop the thread under the needle before pulling the needle and thread through.

Pull the thread firmly to complete the knot in the centre. To finish, take the needle down at **4** and pull the needle and thread through to the back of the fabric.

Seeding

This is produced by working tiny straight stitches at random. They can be large or small, grouped in tight clusters or used sparingly. They produce interesting textures when stitched with different types of thread.

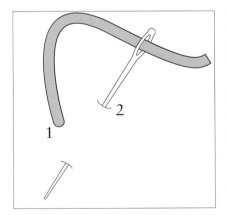

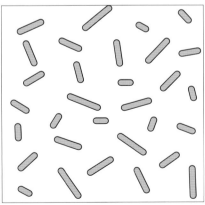

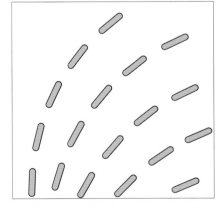

Bring the needle up at **1** and draw the thread through. Take the needle down at **2** and bring it up and out at **3**, ready to start the next stitch.

Seeding can be stitched in a number of different ways – the stitches can be large or small, in tightly knit groups or loose clusters, as shown.

Seeding can also be strung out in a line to resemble running stitch, like the rocket trails in the stunning Fireworks Display picture (page 66).

PROJECT ONE

PRACTICE SAMPLER NO. 3

*T*ry out the stitches featured in this chapter by creating this pretty floral sampler. The pink flowers have clusters of Danish knots at the centre and knotted straight stitches for petals while the smaller blue flowers have a French knot centre and bullion knot petals. Seeding and four-legged knots add texture and colour to the background. The sampler is stitched on evenweave fabric backed with light-weight cotton, but you could use one layer of medium-weight cotton instead if you find this easier.

YOU WILL NEED

At least 15cm (6in) square of 28-count white evenweave fabric sufficient to fit your frame
Light-weight cotton for backing the same size as your evenweave fabric
Anchor Stranded Cotton in light pink 52, deep pink 28, green 225 and blue 145
Milward crewel needle No. 6 and a sharp or between needle
10cm (4in) flexi-hoop
10cm (4in) square of white felt to finish the back
Sylko cotton thread in white for attaching the felt to the back of the framed embroidery

KEY

THREAD
ANCHOR STRANDED COTTON
1 Light Pink 52
2 Deep Pink 28
3 Green 225
4 Blue 145

STITCHES
A Knotted Straight Stitch
B Bullion Knot
C Danish Knots
D French Knot
E Four-legged Knot
F Seeding

STITCH NOTES
The thread colour is indicated by a number and the stitch by a letter.

1 Transfer the design onto the fabric using a soluble pen, transfer pencil or dressmakers' carbon (see pages 12-14). Mount the prepared fabric and backing together in a frame – use an embroidery hoop or 10cm (4in) flexi-hoop.

2 Embroider the flowers first using three strands of Anchor Stranded Cotton in a crewel needle. Then fill the background with seeding using three strands of cotton.

3 If you have stitched the sampler in an embroidery hoop, trim off the excess fabric and mount it in the flexi-hoop. If you have stitched the design in your flexi-hoop, trim the excess fabric to within 12mm (½in) of the frame. Gather in the fabric at the back and cover with felt (see page 30).

CREATIVE OPTIONS

• This is an easy design to convert to a different colour scheme. However, when choosing your colours make sure they stand out against the green seeding in the background – unless you decide to change the colour of the seeding as well.

• The sampler would look just as pretty stitched in Anchor Pearl Cotton No. 5. This is thicker than Anchor Stranded Cotton so you only need one length of thread in the needle.

SCARECROW & FRIEND

*T*his cheerful scarecrow is made from bullion knot straw. His eyes are French
knots and his buttons are worked in four-legged knots. Knotted straight
stitch suggests the standing corn, while seeding adds texture to the ground. He is
outlined in backstitch while the sticks, bird and hat are worked in satin stitch.

YOU WILL NEED

At least 25.5 x 20.5cm (10 x 8in) of 32-count
Charles Craft Irish linen to fit your frame
Cream light-weight cotton for backing the same
size as the linen
Anchor Stranded Cotton in yellow 891, red 13,
blue 168, light brown 339 and dark brown 371
Milward crewel needle No. 6 and a sharp or
between sewing needle
Frame with a 14 x 9cm (5¹/2 x 3¹/2in) aperture
Card mount to fit the frame with an 11 x 6cm
(4¹/4 x 2¹/4in) aperture
Card for lacing to fit the frame
Drima extra-strong thread for lacing

1 Prepare the fabric by transferring the design
onto the fabric using one of the methods on
pages 11-15 such as a transfer pencil or
dressmakers' carbon. Mount the fabric and
backing together in a frame – a rectangular frame
is best for this size of design (see pages 20-23).

2 Embroider all areas using three strands of
Anchor Stranded Cotton in a crewel needle.
Threads should not be taken across the back in
such a way that they can be seen on the right side.
Instead, weave the needle along the back of the
stitches to reach a new stitching point or start a
new thread.

3 On completion remove the embroidery from the
embroidery frame and lightly press it on the
wrong side with a steam iron. Lace the work to the
card using the extra-strong thread (see page 28)
and then mount it in the frame.

FABRIC OPTIONS

This picture is stitched on 32-count Charles Craft Irish
linen and backed with light-weight cotton. If you do
not wish to use two layers of fabric, use one layer of
medium-weight cotton instead.

KEY

THREAD

ANCHOR STRANDED COTTON
1 Yellow 891
2 Red 13
3 Blue 168
4 Light Brown 339
5 Dark Brown 371

STITCH NOTES
The thread colour is
indicated by a number
and the stitch by a letter.
The fine dotted lines
indicate the direction of
the stitch.

STITCHES

A French Knot
B Bullion Knot
C Knotted Straight
Stitch
D Four-legged Knot
E Seeding
F Satin Stitch
(page 33)
G Backstitch
(page 31)

PROJECT THREE

FIREWORKS DISPLAY

*K*not and dot stitches reproduce a stunning display of fireworks in
this unusual picture. Lines of seeding stitch create the firework
trails while bullion knots, knotted straight stitch, French knots and
Danish knots create the fireworks themselves. The clouds are
worked in satin stitch (page 33).

YOU WILL NEED
At least 30.5 x 25.5cm (12 x 10in) of medium-
  weight navy-blue cotton fabric sufficient to fit
  your frame
Anchor Stranded Cotton in white 01, yellow 289,
  pink 52, green 242 and blue 921
Milward crewel needle No. 6 for the embroidery
  and a sharp or between needle for lacing the
  fabric to the card
Frame with an internal aperture 19 x 14cm (7¹/2
  x 5¹/2in)
Card for lacing to fit the frame
Drima extra-strong thread for lacing

1 Transfer the design using a method suitable
for deep-coloured fabric such as dressmakers'
carbon or tacking (see pages 14-15). Mount the
prepared fabric in a frame – a rectangular frame
is best for a fairly large design like this one (see
pages 20-23).

CREATIVE OPTIONS

• This colourful picture is stitched on navy-blue
cotton. If you wish to add a sheen to the sky use a
synthetic fabric instead with a light-weight cotton
backing fabric.

• Feel free to change the colours and thread types
too. Shiny Anchor Marlitt thread or variegated
Bond Multis threads would make the picture look
really lively, or try specialist threads such as
Kreinik gold thread.

2 Stitch all areas using three strands of Anchor
Stranded Cotton in a crewel needle, taking
care not to pull the threads too tight as this can
cause puckering.

3 On completion remove the embroidery from
the frame and lightly press it on the wrong
side with a steam iron. Lace the work to the card
(see page 28) and then mount it in the frame.

KEY

THREAD

ANCHOR STRANDED COTTON

1 White 01
2 Yellow 289
3 Pink 52
4 Green 242
5 Blue 921

STITCHES

A French Knot
B Bullion Knot
C Danish Knot
D Knotted Straight Stitch
E Seeding
F Satin Stitch (page 33)

STITCH NOTES

The thread colour is indicated by a number and the stitch by a letter. The fine dotted lines indicate the direction of the stitch.

MEDIEVAL STRAWBERRY SAMPLER

T his delightful sampler uses a variety of stitches from this and other chapters. It was inspired by a beautiful painting on a French manuscript from the Medieval period and is for the more experienced stitcher.

YOU WILL NEED

Two pieces at least 35.5 x 30.5cm (14 x 12in)
  of light-weight cream cotton fabric
  sufficient to fit your frame
Embroidery threads as listed in the key
Milward crewel needle No. 6 and a sharp or
  between sewing needle
Frame with an internal aperture 24 x 19cm
  (9¹/₂ x 7¹/₂in)
Card for lacing to fit the frame
Wadding the same size as the card
Solid glue stick
Drima extra-strong thread for lacing

1 Transfer the pattern to one piece of fabric using a transfer pencil, or one of the other methods described on pages 11-15. Mount both fabrics together in a frame with the design uppermost – a rectangular frame is best for this size of design (see pages 20-23).

2 Start the embroidery in the centre of the design with the vase. Use three strands of Anchor Stranded Cotton, two strands of Marlitt thread or one strand of Anchor Pearl Cotton as indicated in the key. Take care not to pull the threads too tight as this can cause puckering.

3 On completion remove the embroidery from the frame and lightly press it on the wrong side with a steam iron. Glue the wadding to the card and lace the embroidery on top (see page 28), then mount the embroidery in your frame.

COLOUR OPTIONS

This project is stitched on two layers of light-weight cream cotton. You could use 32-count Charles Craft cream Irish linen for the top layer if you prefer, but you will still need a light-weight cotton backing.

KEY

THREAD

ANCHOR STRANDED COTTON
1 Yellow 297
2 Gold 901
3 Dark Red 19
4 Light Green 226
5 Dark Green 230
6 Blue 133
7 Brown 905
8 Orange 330, Cherry 335 and Dark Red 19 (one strand of each colour)

ANCHOR MARLITT THREAD
9 White 800
10 Gold 1078
11 Green 1030
12 Blue 835

ANCHOR PEARL COTTON NO. 5
13 Gold 307
14 Blue 147

STITCHES

A French Knot
B Knotted Straight Stitch
C Satin Stitch (page 33)
D Blanket Stitch (page 33)
E Stem Stitch (page 46)
F Backstitch (page 31)
G Lazy-daisy Stitch (page 32)
H Trellis Filling Stitch (page 89)

STITCH NOTES

The thread colour is indicated by a number and the stitch by a letter. The fine dotted lines indicate the direction of the stitch.

CHAPTER FIVE

CHAINS & LOOPS

*T*he chain and loop family is a very versatile set of stitches which can be used in
a variety of ways, as borders, outlines, filling stitches and isolated stitches. Try
using this family in all these different ways when you stitch the charming Ginger-bread
House (page 78) and Summer Bouquet (page 83). Or see how chains and loops can
be used to make patterns by working the Decorative Wall Hanging (page 80).

The six stitches in the chain and loop family are chain stitch, cable chain stitch, closed
buttonhole stitch, blanket stitch wheels, lazy-daisy stitch and long-tailed daisy stitch.
This family is very versatile: while cable and closed buttonhole stitch make
interesting borders, chain stitch is a useful outline stitch.

Lazy-daisy Stitch

This quick-and-easy stitch is very useful for floral designs. A single stitch looks like a leaf or you can group several stitches around a central point to suggest a daisy flower.

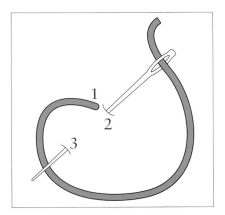
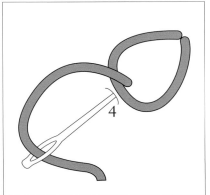
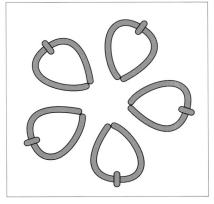

Bring the needle through at **1**. Insert the needle at **2** and bring it back up at **3**, making sure the thread runs underneath the needle, as shown.

Draw the needle through, take it over the looped thread and insert it at **4**, as shown. When the needle is drawn through at the back the loop is secured.

A lazy-daisy stitch can be worked either as a single stitch or in a small cluster radiating from a central point to suggest a pretty daisy flower.

Chain Stitch

A popular stitch, chain stitch belongs to both the chain and outline stitch families. It is quick and easy to work and forms a textured line made up of interlocking loops which resembles a chain. Chain stitch can be worked on a straight or curved line.

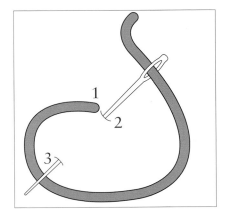
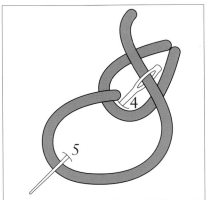
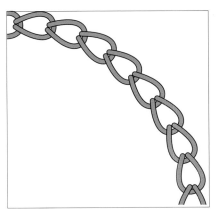

Start by bringing the needle through at **1**. Insert the needle at **2** and bring it back up at **3**, making sure the thread runs under the needle, as shown.

Draw the needle through to finish the stitch. Now take the needle down at **4** (beside **3**) and bring it up at **5** with the thread looped under the needle.

By repeating this sequence you can create a chain of stitches. Chain stitch is very versatile and can be stitched straight, curved or coiled, as shown.

Cable Chain Stitch

This stitch can be used to create a decorative outline or border. It is made up of a line of chain stitches separated by a series of short bars which resemble the links in a chain. The bar and chain are made at the same time.

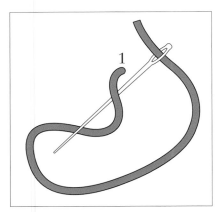

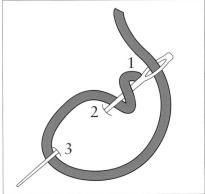

Bring the needle up and draw the thread out at **1**. Wind the thread round the needle by taking it up and over, round and then under the needle.

Insert the needle at **2** (the gap between **1** and **2** determines the length of the bar) and bring it up at **3** with the thread looped under the needle.

Repeat the sequence, starting by winding the thread round the needle to form a line of chains and bars. Make sure that the spacing is even.

Closed Buttonhole Stitch

This variation of blanket stitch (page 33) produces a row of evenly spaced triangular loops. Like blanket stitch it can be worked on a straight or curved line and it makes a pretty border stitch.

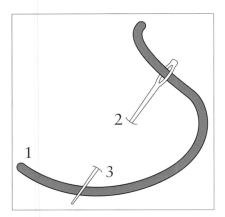

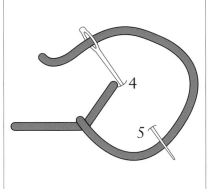

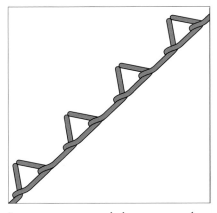

Start by bringing the needle up and out at **1**. Take the needle down at **2** and bring it out at **3**, looping the thread under the needle before drawing it through.

Form the triangular loop by taking the needle down at **4** (close to **2**) and bringing it up at **5**, in line with **3**. The thread should be looped under the needle.

Leave a space and then repeat the sequence from **2** to **5** to create a series of evenly spaced triangles. Do not pull the thread too tight as this can cause puckering.

Blanket Stitch Wheels

Like closed buttonhole stitch, this is a variation of blanket stitch (page 33). The wheels are quick and easy to stitch and form decorative circles which are useful for depicting flower centres.

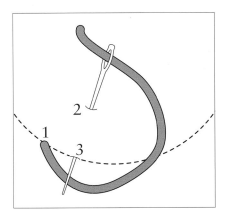 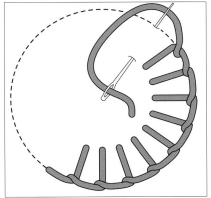 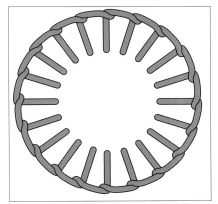

Bring the needle up and out at **1**. Take the needle down at **2** and bring it back out at **3**, looping the thread under the needle before drawing it through.

Following the curve of the circle, repeat the movement with evenly spaced stitches. Do not pull the thread too tightly as this can cause puckering.

Continue round to the starting point. When you have completed the circle, take the needle down and fasten the thread at the back to finish.

Long-tailed Daisy Stitch

This intriguing stitch is made up of straight stitch and lazy-daisy stitch. It can be used as an isolated stitch or worked in clusters. It is useful for forming both flower centres and petals.

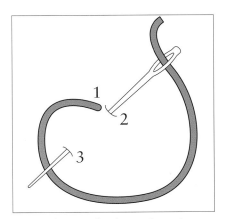 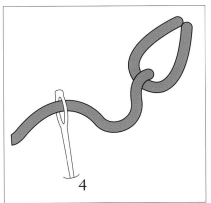 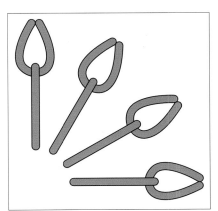

Bring the needle through at **1**. Insert the needle at **2** and bring it up at **3**, making sure the thread runs under the needle, as shown.

Form the straight stitch by inserting the needle at **4**. Take the needle and thread through the fabric to complete the stitch.

The length of the straight stitch can be easily adjusted. Work long-tailed daisy stitch as an isolated stitch or in clusters, as shown.

PROJECT ONE

PRACTICE SAMPLER NO. 4

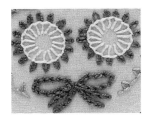

*T*his pretty picture uses all the stitches in this chapter, making it an ideal
practice sampler. It is designed to show the different ways in which this
family can be stitched – for borders, outlines and fillings, in clusters and isolated
stitches. Closed buttonhole stitch creates the border, cable chain stitch produces the leaf
outlines, chain stitch fills the pretty bow, a cluster of long-tailed daisy stitches creates
the blue flower and isolated lazy-daisy stitches around each blanket
stitch wheel make up the purple flowers.

YOU WILL NEED
At least 15cm (6in) square of medium-weight
  green cotton fabric sufficient to fit your frame
Light-weight cotton backing the same size as the
  green fabric
Anchor Pearl Cotton No. 5 in yellow 891, brown
  363, green 226, blue 131 and violet 100
Milward crewel needle No. 6 and a sharp or
  between needle
10cm (4in) flexi-hoop
10cm (4in) square of white felt to finish the back
Sylko cotton thread in white

KEY

THREAD

ANCHOR PEARL COTTON NO.5

1 Yellow 891
2 Brown 363
3 Green 226
4 Blue 131
5 Violet 100

STITCHES

A Lazy-daisy Stitch
B Chain Stitch
C Cable Chain Stitch
D Blanket Stitch Wheel
E Closed Buttonhole
Stitch
F Long-tailed Daisy
Stitch

STITCH NOTES

The thread colour is
indicated by a number
and the stitch by a letter.

1 Transfer the design onto the fabric using a soluble pen, transfer pencil or dressmakers' carbon (see pages 11-14). Mount the prepared fabric and backing together in a frame – use an embroidery hoop or 10cm (4in) flexi-hoop.

2 Embroider the flowers first using one strand of Anchor Pearl Cotton in a crewel needle. When all the flowers have been worked stitch the outer border and bow.

3 If you have stitched the sampler in an embroidery hoop, trim the fabric to measure 15cm (6in) and mount it in the flexi-hoop. If you

have stitched the design in your flexi-hoop, trim the excess fabric to within 12mm (½in) of the frame. Gather in the fabric at the back and cover with felt (see page 30).

COLOUR OPTIONS

This is an easy design to convert to a different colour scheme but when choosing your colours make sure they stand out against the green background. Of course, you could always change the colour of the background as well.

PROJECT TWO

GINGER-BREAD HOUSE

his delightful house incorporates many of the stitches from this chapter but it also has satin stitch windows, blanket stitch shutters and backstitch contours. The smoke rising from the chimney is worked in seeding.

YOU WILL NEED

At least 25.5cm (10in) square of 32-count Charles Craft Irish linen to fit your frame
Cream light-weight cotton backing the same size as the linen
Anchor Stranded Cotton in yellow 891, red 39, green 261, blue 176 and brown 349
Milward crewel needle No. 6 to work the embroidery and a sharp or between needle to lace the embroidery to the frame

Frame with a 14cm (5½in) square aperture
Card and wadding to fit the frame
Strong thread for lacing
Solid glue stick
Cardboard mount to fit the frame with an 11cm (4¼in) circular aperture
18cm (7in) square of cotton fabric for covering the mount
Repositionable spray glue and masking tape

KEY

THREAD

ANCHOR STRANDED COTTON

1 Yellow 891
2 Red 39
3 Green 261
4 Blue 176
5 Brown 349

STITCHES

A Blanket Stitch Wheels
B Chain Stitch
C Cable Chain Stitch
D Closed Buttonhole Stitch
E Long-tailed Daisy Stitch
F Seeding (page 61)
G Satin Stitch (page 33)
H Backstitch (page 31)
J Blanket Stitch (page 33)

STITCH NOTES

The thread colour is indicated by a number and the stitch by a letter. The fine dotted lines indicate the direction of the stitch.

1 Transfer the design onto the fabric using any of the methods on pages 11-15. Mount the prepared fabric and backing together in a frame (see pages 20-23).

2 Embroider all areas using two strands of Anchor Stranded Cotton in a crewel needle. Threads should not be taken across the back in such a way that they can be seen on the right side. Instead, weave the needle along the back of the stitches to reach a new stitching position.

3 On completion remove the embroidery from the frame and lightly press it on the wrong side with a steam iron. Trim it to size as necessary. Glue the wadding to the card and lace the embroidery on top (see page 28). Cover the mount with fabric and fit the laced embroidery and mount in the frame.

FABRIC OPTIONS

This picture is stitched on Charles Craft Irish linen and backed with light-weight cotton. If you don't wish to use two layers of fabric you could use just one layer of medium-weight cotton.

COLOUR OPTIONS

This is an easy design to convert to different colours. If you are stitching this for a child's bedroom or playroom you could easily match it to the room's colour scheme. Choose the fabric colour you want first, then take the fabric with you when you select the embroidery threads. Hold all the threads together against the fabric to check that they combine well and create the effect you want.

DECORATIVE WALL HANGING

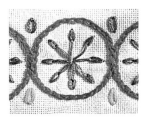

*T*his striking wall hanging is worked in five of the six stitches

from this chapter. You can make it as long as you like – just

repeat the design. Use the colours given in the key or choose your

own colour combination to suit a particular room scheme.

YOU WILL NEED

At least 28 x 20.5cm (11 x 8in) square of 28-
  count evenweave Lineve to fit your frame
White medium-weight cotton backing the same
  size as the evenweave fabric
Anchor Stranded Cotton in yellow 303, red 13,
  green 239, blue 131 and lilac 98
Milward crewel needle No. 6 and a sharp or
  between needle
15cm (6in) hanging supports
Sylko cotton thread to match your fabric

1 Transfer the design onto the fabric using any
of the methods on pages 11-15. Mount the
prepared fabric in a frame – a rectangular frame
is ideal (see pages 20-23).

2 Start the embroidery at the top of the design
using four strands of Anchor Stranded Cotton
in a crewel needle.

3 On completion remove the embroidery from
the frame and lightly press it on the wrong
side with a steam iron. Trim to size, if required.
Pin the embroidery and backing fabrics together
with right sides facing. Machine stitch the sides –
the line of stitching should be at the edge of the
embroidery. Remove the pins and turn the work
right sides out.

4 Turn 2.5cm (1in) over at the top and bottom
to form the loops for the supports and
slipstitch in place. Lightly press with a steam iron
and assemble on the hanging supports following
the manufacturer's instructions.

> **FABRIC OPTIONS**
>
> This hanging has been worked on evenweave Lineve
> but you could use 32-count Charles Craft Irish linen
> or medium-weight cotton fabric instead.

KEY

THREAD

ANCHOR STRANDED COTTON

1 Yellow 303
2 Red 13
3 Green 239
4 Blue 131
5 Lilac 98

STITCHES

A Chain Stitch
B Cable Chain Stitch
C Long-tailed Daisy Stitch
D Lazy-daisy Stitch
E Closed Buttonhole Stitch

STITCH NOTES

The thread colour is indicated by a number and the stitch by a letter.

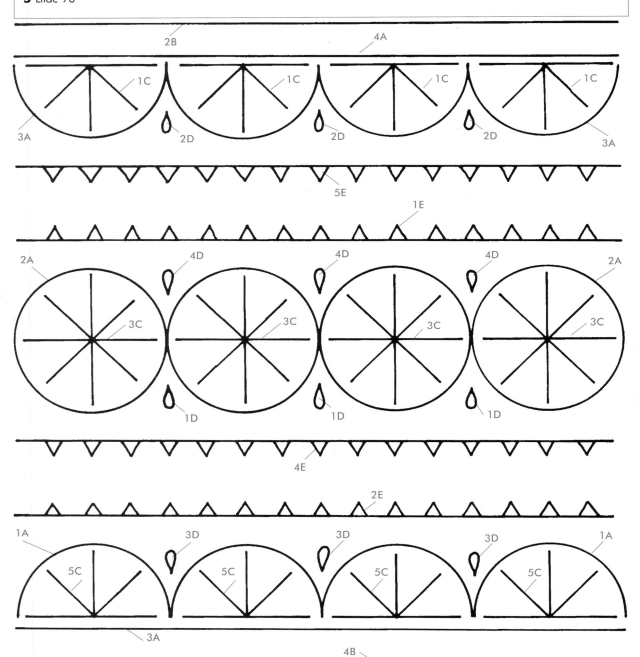

PROJECT FOUR

SUMMER BOUQUET

*S*titch this delightful bouquet and have flowers in your home all year round. The
petals are worked in lazy-daisy stitch and long-tailed daisy stitch with French
knot centres, while the stems and leaves are worked in stem stitch and chain stitch.
Follow the colours shown or change them to create a bouquet as a gift –
for a ruby or golden wedding anniversary, for example.

YOU WILL NEED

*Two pieces at least 35.5 x 30.5cm (14 x 12in) of
light-weight cream cotton fabric sufficient to
fit your frame*

*Anchor Stranded Cotton in beige 874, light green
261 and dark green 262*

*Anchor Marlitt thread in light pink 1069, deep
pink 815, medium lilac 857 and dark lilac 858*

*Milward crewel needle No. 6 and a sharp or
between needle*

Ribbon bow

*Frame with an internal aperture 24 x 19cm
(9½ x 7½in)*

Card for lacing to fit the frame

Drima extra-strong thread for lacing

*Mount with an internal aperture 19 x 14cm
(7½ x 5½in)*

1 Transfer the design onto one fabric piece using
a transfer pen or any of the other methods on
pages 11-15. Mount the prepared fabrics in a
rectangular frame with the design uppermost (see
pages 20-23).

2 Start the embroidery in the centre of the
design, using three strands of Anchor
Stranded Cotton or two strands of Anchor
Marlitt thread. Take care not to pull the threads
too tight as this can cause puckering.

3 On completion remove the embroidery from
the frame and lightly press it on the wrong
side with a steam iron. Add the ribbon bow. Lace
the work to the card (see page 28) and then
mount it in the frame.

KEY

THREAD

ANCHOR STRANDED COTTON

1 Beige 874
2 Light Green 261
3 Dark Green 262

ANCHOR MARLITT THREAD

4 Light Pink 1069
5 Deep Pink 815
6 Medium Lilac 857
7 Dark Lilac 858

STITCHES

A Lazy-daisy Stitch
B Chain Stitch
C Cable Chain Stitch
D Long-tailed Daisy
Stitch
E Stem Stitch (page 46)
F Satin Stitch (page 33)
G French Knot
(page 32)
H Trellis Filling
Stitch (page 89)

STITCH NOTES

The thread colour is
indicated by a number
and the stitch by a letter.

HANDY HINTS

Large projects are
very prone to
puckering so use
either a roller frame
or stretchers for
mounting this work.
These frames hold the
fabric firmly.

CHAPTER SIX

SOLID & OPEN FILLINGS

*T*his family of stitches is used to fill the interior of a design in various different
ways, as the projects in this chapter show. The attractive Riverside Cushion
(page 94) uses only solid fillings such as satin stitch while the Stone Shop picture (page
92) is stitched in decorative open fillings like trellis filling stitch. The Blue & Gold
Floral Picture (page 97) incorporates both styles of filling stitches.

*The six stitches featured in the filling family have been split into two groups –
solid and open fillings. The three stitches in the solid fillings group are satin stitch,
split filling stitch and fishbone stitch, while the three open filling stitches
are blanket filling stitch, trellis filling stitch and couched filling stitch.*

Satin Stitch

This is the easiest filling stitch and the most versatile of the solid fillings. Although satin stitch is usually worked as a set of parallel lines, the stitches are easily fanned, which makes it a useful stitch for flower petals.

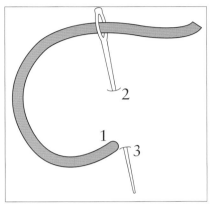

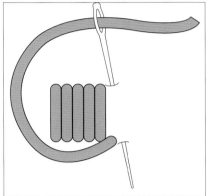

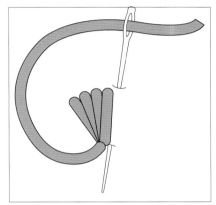

Bring the needle up at **1** and pull the thread through. Go down at **2** and bring the needle back out at **3**, next to **1**. Pull the thread through to form the first stitch.

Repeat the first sequence to create a set of parallel stitches. The tension is very important with this stitch – if the stitches are pulled too tight puckering can occur.

Satin stitch can also be angled to produce a fan shape. This is formed by bringing the needle through the same hole at the base of the fan, as shown.

Split Filling Stitch

This filling stitch is useful for covering large areas where satin stitch would not be suitable. The first couple of rows can look untidy but as you add more the filling takes on an attractive woven appearance.

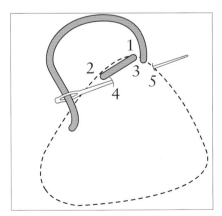

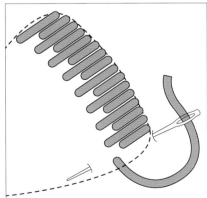

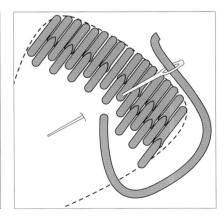

Bring the needle up at **1**, take it down at **2** and draw it up and out at **3**. Now go down at **4** and come up and out at **5**.

Work a series of long and short stitches by repeating the process. At the end of the row bring the needle up ready for the next row.

Repeat the sequence, working in reverse on alternate rows, but pass the needle through the stitch above, splitting the thread.

Fishbone Stitch

This stitch is excellent for foliage, producing a padded ridge where stitches overlap at the centre which looks like the central vein in a leaf. This stitch is used for the leaves of the bulrushes on the Riverside Cushion (page 94).

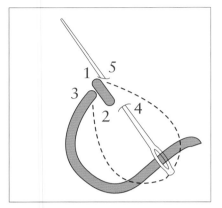

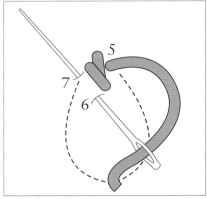

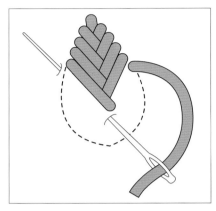

Work one straight stitch in the centre by bringing the needle up at **1** and taking it down at **2**. Come up at **3**, take the needle down at **4** and come up and out at **5**.

Take the thread down and across the bottom of the previous stitch by inserting the needle at **6** (which is to the left of **4**) then bring the needle up and out at **7**.

Form the fishbone pattern by repeating the sequence from **3** to **6**. The stitches can be worked between parallel lines or gently fanned to form a leaf shape.

Blanket Filling Stitch

This is a variation of blanket stitch (page 33) produced by overlapping rows of blanket stitches which have been worked in pairs. As well as being a very attractive decorative filling stitch it is also excellent for representing basketwork in an embroidery.

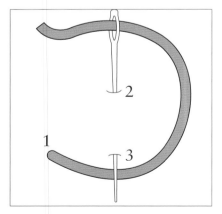

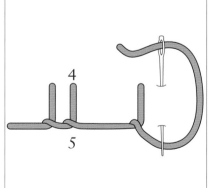

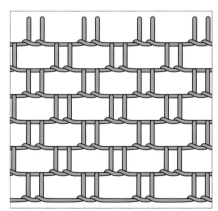

Bring the needle up and out at **1**. Take the needle down at **2** and up at **3**. Make sure the thread passes under the needle before pulling the needle through to form the first stitch.

Insert the needle at **4** and come up at **5**, making sure the loop goes under the needle; draw the needle through. Leave a space and repeat from **2** to **5** to form the first row of stitching.

Create the wicker-like pattern by staggering the blanket-stitch pairs in each row so that the stitches in even-numbered rows fall beneath and between the stitches in odd-numbered rows.

Trellis Filling Stitch

This pretty open filling stitch is widely used in crewelwork. It looks particularly attractive when stitched in different colour combinations with the trellis lines stitched in one thread and the bars worked in another.

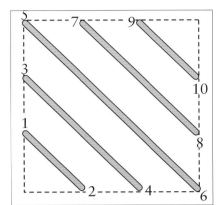

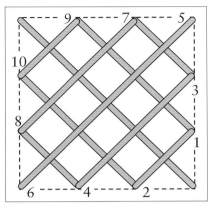

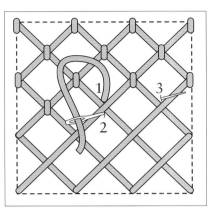

Lay down a series of diagonal lines by spanning the area to be stitched with individual straight stitches. Make sure the spaces between the stitches are even, as shown.

Lay down a second series of diagonal lines which cross the first set to form small diamond-shaped trellis. Again, care is needed to make sure that the spacing is even.

Secure each crossing point of the trellis with a short vertical stitch (bar). To form a bar bring the needle up at **1**, then down at **2** and back up at **3**.

Couched Filling Stitch

Once widely used in Jacobean laidwork, this decorative stitch remains a popular crewelwork stitch. It is worked in a similar way to trellis filling stitch but the lattice is formed by a series of horizontal and vertical lines secured with small crosses.

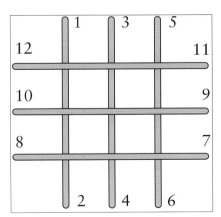

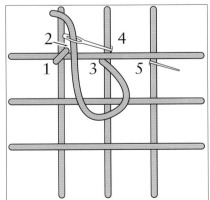

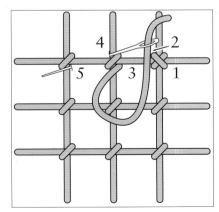

Form the lattice by laying down a series of vertical stitches and then cross these with a set of horizontal stitches. The crossing lines should form a series of evenly spaced square boxes.

Secure the lattice by coming up and out at **1**. Go over the lattice and down at **2**, bringing the needle up and out at **3** at the next intersection. Repeat by going down at **4** and coming up at **5**.

Stitch a series of diagonal lines that cross over the first set. Come up and out at **1**; take the thread over the lattice, down at **2** and up at **3**. Repeat by going down at **4** and coming up at **5**.

PROJECT ONE

PRACTICE SAMPLER NO. 5

*A*ll six filling stitches feature on this colourful practice sampler. The design is stitched on synthetic fabric so you will need a second layer of light-weight cotton backing to help prevent puckering. Alternatively, if you wish to work with one layer of fabric, choose a medium-weight cotton fabric which does not require a backing.

YOU WILL NEED

At least 15cm (6in) square of white synthetic fabric sufficient to fit your frame

White light-weight cotton backing fabric the same size as the synthetic fabric

Anchor Stranded Cotton in gold 311, bronze 347, lilac 85, green 206 and blue 120

Milward crewel needle No. 6 and a sharp or between needle

10cm (4in) flexi-hoop

10cm (4in) square of white felt to finish the back of the frame

Sylko sewing cotton in white

HANDY HINTS

Solid filling stitches are very prone to puckering, so make sure you secure your fabric firmly in your frame and adjust it from time to time, as necessary.

---

1 Transfer the design to the fabric using one of the methods on pages 11-15 suitable for synthetics. A soluble pen or dressmakers' carbon works well as the design won't take long to complete. Mount the prepared fabric in a frame – you can either use an embroidery hoop or mount the fabric in your 10cm (4in) flexi-hoop (see pages 20-23 and 30).

2 Use two strands of Anchor Stranded Cotton in a crewel needle to work blanket filling stitch in the centre of the bronze leaf. Fill the small blue flower in trellis filling stitch using two strands of blue and one strand of lilac. Fill the pink flower in trellis filling stitch with two strands of bronze and one strand of blue.

For the remaining stitches use three strands of Anchor Stranded Cotton in a crewel needle, taking care not to pull the stitches too tight as this may cause puckering.

3 On completion remove the sampler from the frame and lightly press it on the wrong side with a steam iron to remove any slight puckers from the fabric.

4 If you have stitched the design in an embroidery hoop, trim off the excess fabric and mount the work in the flexi-hoop. If you have stitched the design in your flexi-hoop, trim the excess fabric to within 12mm (½in) of the frame. Gather in the fabric at the back and cover with felt (see page 30).

Note: the finished sampler is shown on page 86.

HANDY HINTS

If you wish to use a synthetic fabric but do not want to use a separate backing fabric, substitute the cotton backing for a medium-weight iron-on interfacing. Lay the interfacing glue-side down on the back of the synthetic fabric, making sure it is centred. Secure by lightly pressing with a steam iron.

KEY

THREAD

ANCHOR STRANDED COTTON

1 Gold 311
2 Bronze 347
3 Lilac 85
4 Green 206
5 Blue 120

STITCHES

A Satin Stitch
B Split Filling Stitch
C Fishbone Stitch
D Blanket Filling Stitch
E Trellis Filling Stitch
F Couched Filling Stitch

STITCH NOTES

The thread colour is indicated by a number and the stitch by a letter. The fine dotted lines indicate the direction of the stitch.

PROJECT TWO

STONE SHOP

A mixture of open filling stitches – blanket filling stitch, couched filling
stitch and trellis filling stitch – was used to decorate this
building's roof, walls and shop front.

YOU WILL NEED

At least 25.5 x 20.5cm (10 x 8in) of medium-
weight cotton sufficient to fit your frame
Anchor Stranded Cotton in pale pink 376,
medium pink 378, light grey 398 and
medium grey 399
Frame with a 9 x 14cm (3½ x 5½in) aperture

Milward crewel needle No. 6 and a sharp or
between needle
Card for lacing to fit the frame
Wadding the same size as the card
Solid glue stick
Drima extra-strong thread for lacing

KEY

THREAD

ANCHOR STRANDED COTTON

1 Pale Pink 376 and
Light Grey 398 (two
strands of each colour)
2 Medium Pink 378 and
Medium Grey 399 (two
strands of each colour)

STITCHES
A Blanket Filling Stitch
B Couched Filling Stitch
C Trellis Filling Stitch
D Backstitch (page 31)
E Satin Stitch (page 33)

STITCH NOTES
The thread colour is
indicated by a number
and the stitch by a letter.

1 Transfer your design to the fabric (see pages 11-15) and mount it, together with the backing, in a frame (see pages 20-23).

2 Use two strands of each colour indicated in the key so that you have four strands of thread in the crewel needle. Work the backstitch outline first, in the colours shown, before stitching the decorative fillings.

3 Work the open filling stitches, taking care not to pull the thread too tight as this could cause permanent puckering.

4 On completion remove the embroidery from the frame and lightly press it on the wrong side with a steam iron. Glue the wadding to the card and lace the embroidery on top (see page 28), then mount the embroidery in your frame.

CREATIVE OPTIONS

Part of the charm of this project lies in its subtle blend of threads. Although you can create endless colour combinations with Anchor Stranded Cotton, the project would also look attractive stitched in Bond Multis variegated threads.

PROJECT THREE

RIVERSIDE CUSHION

*T*his delightful scene features mallard ducks worked in split filling stitch with beaks of satin stitch and French knot eyes. They are swimming among bulrushes and leaves worked in satin stitch, stem stitch and fishbone stitch. The ripples on the water are defined with backstitch. This design is worked for a cushion cover, but it would also make a beautiful picture when framed. It is a project for the more experienced stitcher.

YOU WILL NEED

Two pieces at least 48cm (19in) square of medium-weight cream cotton sufficient to fit your frame

Anchor Stranded Cotton in the colours listed in the key

Milward crewel needle No. 6 and a sharp or between needle

46cm (18in) square cushion pad

Sylko cotton thread to match the fabric

HANDY HINTS

• Solid fillings are prone to puckering so it is advisable to use a rectangular frame for mounting this work. This holds the fabric more firmly than a circular hoop.

• This design was worked on buff-coloured medium-weight curtain fabric but you could use a medium/heavy-weight dressmaking cotton.

1 Transfer the design to the fabric using a suitable method such as tacking (see pages 11-15). Mount the prepared fabric in a rectangular frame (see pages 20-23).

2 Using four strands of thread in a crewel needle, stitch the ducks first. Take care not to pull the threads too tightly as this could cause puckering.

3 On completion remove the embroidery from the frame and lightly press it on the wrong side with a steam iron.

4 To make the cushion lay the design right-side down on the backing fabric and pin. Machine a 12mm (½in) seam round three sides, leaving the bottom open. Turn the cover to the right side, press and insert the pad. Turn in the fabric at the bottom and slipstitch to finish.

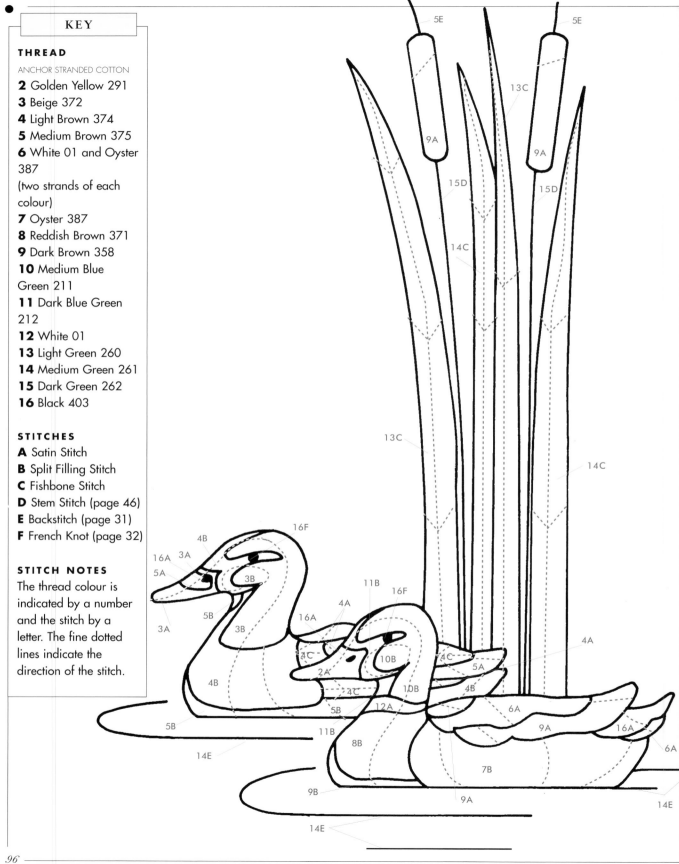

KEY

THREAD

ANCHOR STRANDED COTTON

2 Golden Yellow 291
3 Beige 372
4 Light Brown 374
5 Medium Brown 375
6 White 01 and Oyster 387
(two strands of each colour)
7 Oyster 387
8 Reddish Brown 371
9 Dark Brown 358
10 Medium Blue Green 211
11 Dark Blue Green 212
12 White 01
13 Light Green 260
14 Medium Green 261
15 Dark Green 262
16 Black 403

STITCHES

A Satin Stitch
B Split Filling Stitch
C Fishbone Stitch
D Stem Stitch (page 46)
E Backstitch (page 31)
F French Knot (page 32)

STITCH NOTES

The thread colour is indicated by a number and the stitch by a letter. The fine dotted lines indicate the direction of the stitch.

BLUE & GOLD FLORAL PICTURE

illing stitches, especially open filling stitches, are usually associated with crewelwork. In this picture both solid and open filling stitches are used to produce a modern crewelwork design. The gentle sheen of Anchor Stranded Cottons mixed with the sparkle of Anchor Marlitt threads and gold thread give this picture a luxurious finish.

YOU WILL NEED

At least 35.5 x 30.5cm (14 x 12in) of medium-weight cotton sufficient to fit your frame

Anchor Stranded Cotton in pale blue 128, medium blue 130 and dark blue 146

Anchor Marlitt thread in pale blue 1059 and medium blue 1009

Anchor Lamé stranded thread in gold 300

Milward crewel needle No. 6 and a fine, sharp-pointed needle for couching

Frame with an internal aperture of 24 x 19cm (9^1/$_2$ x 7^1/$_2$in)

Card to fit the frame

Blue mount with an internal aperture 20.5 x 15cm (8 x 6in)

1 Transfer the design to the fabric using one of the methods on pages 11-15. Mount the prepared fabric in a frame – a rectangular one is best for a project of this size (see pages 20-23).

2 Using three strands of Anchor Stranded Cotton or two strands of Anchor Marlitt thread, work the flower petals and fillings first and then the stems and leaves. When working couched filling stitch use gold thread for the lattice work and medium blue Anchor Marlitt thread for the crosses. When working trellis filling stitch use medium blue Anchor Stranded Cotton for the lattice and gold for the bars. Where gold thread is used in the fillings use all the strands. Use all the strands of gold thread for couching and one strand of gold thread to secure the line. Take care not to pull the threads too tightly as this could cause puckering.

3 On completion remove the embroidery from the frame and lightly press it on the wrong side with a steam iron. Lace the work to the card (see page 28) and then place it in the frame behind the mount.

KEY

THREAD

ANCHOR STRANDED COTTON
1 Pale Blue 128
2 Medium Blue 130
3 Dark Blue 146

ANCHOR MARLITT THREAD
4 Pale Blue 1059

5 Medium Blue 1009

ANCHOR LAMÉ STRANDED
6 Gold 300

STITCHES
A Satin Stitch
B Fishbone Filling Stitch

C Blanket Stitch (page 33)
D Couched Filling Stitch
E Trellis Filling Stitch
F Blanket Filling Stitch
G Stem Stitch (page 46)
H Backstitch (page 31)
J Couching (page 46)

STITCH NOTES
The thread colour is indicated by a number and the stitch by a letter. The fine dotted lines indicate the direction of the stitch.

CHAPTER SEVEN

BORDERS AND BANDS

*M*ost stitches in this group are worked on a straight line and form
a perfect decorative finish for such items as table-cloths, tray cloths
and cushion covers. However, as the Oriental Vase project on page 110 shows, these
stitches can be used in a variety of ways, even to create a stylish picture.

The six stitches in this chapter have been chosen for their simplicity and versatility.
Three of them come from the feather stitch family and range from a simple
open loop to a very decorative feathered chain stitch. Chinese stitch,
chevron stitch and blanket stitch are also featured on the following pages.

Blanket Stitch

This versatile stitch can be evenly spaced, as shown, or worked without gaps to form a solid band. The vertical lines can be stitched at varying heights which is particularly useful for representing grass. The line of stitching can also be curved to form a circle (see page 75).

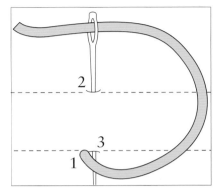
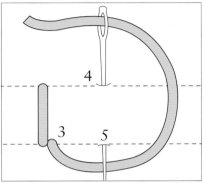
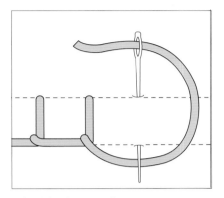

Create one straight stitch to start the line neatly by bringing the needle up through the fabric at **1**. Go down at **2** and come up at **3** (which is immediately to the side of **1**).

Leave the required space and take the needle down at **4** and up at **5**, with the thread running behind the needle. Draw the needle through the fabric to form the stitch.

The blanket stitch pattern is formed by repeating this sequence. Try not to pull too tightly when drawing the thread through as this may cause puckering.

Chevron Stitch

This stitch can either be worked as a single line to form a border, or in repeat rows to create an interesting filling stitch. The repeated rows form an attractive diamond pattern. This stitch is also popular in smocking. Although chevron stitch does not work well on curves the stitch height and width can be adjusted easily.

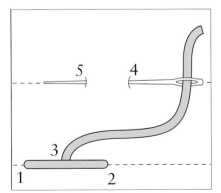
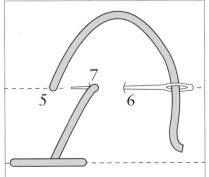
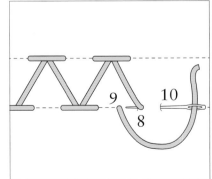

Bring the needle up at **1**, down at **2** and up at **3** (halfway between **1** and **2**), taking care not to split the horizontal stitch. Insert the needle at **4** and draw it out at **5**.

Take the needle down at **6** and up at **7** (halfway between **5** and **6**), taking care not to split the horizontal stitch when the needle comes up in the centre.

Go down at **8** and up at **9** and pull the needle through. Insert the needle at **10** and come up at **8**. Repeat the sequence from inserting the needle at **4**.

Chinese Stitch

This can be used both as a decorative border stitch and as a filling stitch.
The filling stitch is created by repeating rows of stitching to form a wave-like pattern
as in the Oriental Vase picture (page 110). Although this stitch can be worked on
ordinary cottons it is easier to stitch on evenweave fabrics such as Aida.

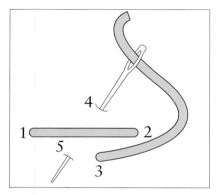
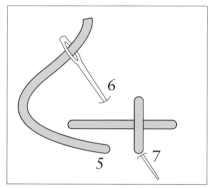
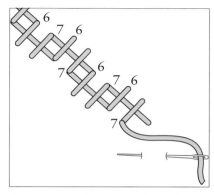

Come up at **1**, go down at **2**, come up at **3** and pull the thread through. Take the thread across the horizontal stitch, go down at **4** and come up at **5**.

Take the thread across the horizontal stitch once again. Go down at **6** and come up at **7** which is the starting point for the next sequence of stitches.

Repeat by raising and lowering the horizontal stitches as shown above. The position of **7** will change according to the position of the next horizontal stitch.

Feather Stitch

This stitch is made up of a series of V-shaped loops which alternate from side to side. It is an excellent
stitch for working curved lines and for this reason it is useful for joining fabric in crazy patchwork.

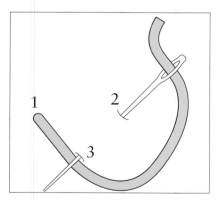
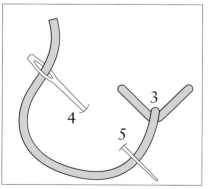
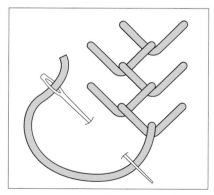

To make the first V-shaped loop, bring the needle up at **1**, take it down at **2** and up again at **3**, taking care that the thread is positioned behind the needle.

Pull the thread through and go down at **4**. Come up again at **5**, taking care that the thread is behind the needle, to form a second V-shaped loop.

Continue to work the open loop but alternate from side to side as shown in the diagram to form the distinctive, airy shape of the feather stitch.

Double Feather Stitch

This is a variation on the basic feather stitch described opposite and is formed by adding an extra V-shaped loop to each side of the embroidery. It is a useful stitch for creating feathery foliage for a floral design and is also a popular stitch for smocking.

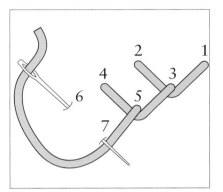

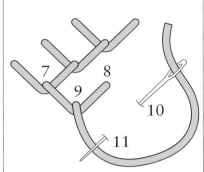

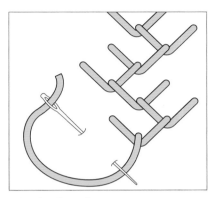

Follow the instructions for feather stitch, below left, from **1–5**. Then go down at **6** and come up at **7** to form the third stitch in the diagonal row.

The diagonal row now turns right. Go down at **8** and bring the needle up at **9**. Repeat again by going down at **10** and coming up at **11**.

The feathered appearance is formed by repeating this sequence of stitches. Take care not to pull threads too tightly as this may cause puckering.

Feathered Chain Stitch

This highly decorative stitch is suitable for wide borders. Although it can be worked on plain-weave fabrics it is easier to work on evenweaves.

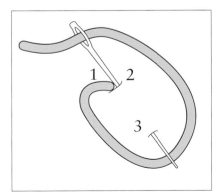

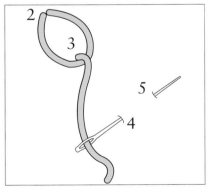

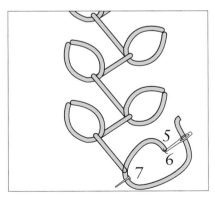

Form the basic chain stitch by bringing the needle up at **1** and going down at **2** (which is by the side of **1**). Bring the needle out at **3** and draw the thread through.

Take the needle down at **4** and up at **5**. This completes one stitch and places the needle in the correct position to work the next stitch to the right.

A chain is formed on the other side by going down at **6** and coming up at **7**. Continue this sequence to form the pattern shown above.

PRACTICE SAMPLER No. 6

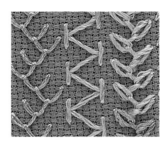

*T*his practice sampler is easy to sew, allowing you to practise
the stitches in this chapter. You can either frame it to make
a pretty picture or keep it as a useful reference guide to the stitches.
Although it could be worked on plain material you will find it is
much easier to stitch on an evenweave fabric such as Aida.

YOU WILL NEED

25.5 x 20.5cm (10 x 8in) 14-count green Aida
Bond Multis Springtime 07000–4
Anchor Marlitt thread in lilac pink 813
Milward tapestry needle
Picture frame with a 9 x 14cm (3¹/₂ x 5¹/₂in)
  rectangular aperture
Card for lacing to fit the frame
Wadding to fit the card
Solid glue stick
Drima extra-strong thread for lacing

1 Mount the Aida in a circular or rectangular
frame (see pages 20-23). For information on
working from a chart see page 18.

2 Start at the top of the fabric with the blanket
stitch border and then work all the vertical
rows, finishing with the horizontal chevron border
at the bottom.

Work the following stitches in Bond Multis
thread: blanket stitch, Chinese stitch, chevron
stitch and feathered chain stitch.

Use the Anchor Marlitt rayon thread to work
the feather stitch and double feather stitch rows.
Rayon thread divides into four strands – use all
four strands in the needle when stitching.

3 On completion remove the work from the
frame and lightly press on the wrong side.
Mount the sampler in your chosen frame (see
pages 27-30).

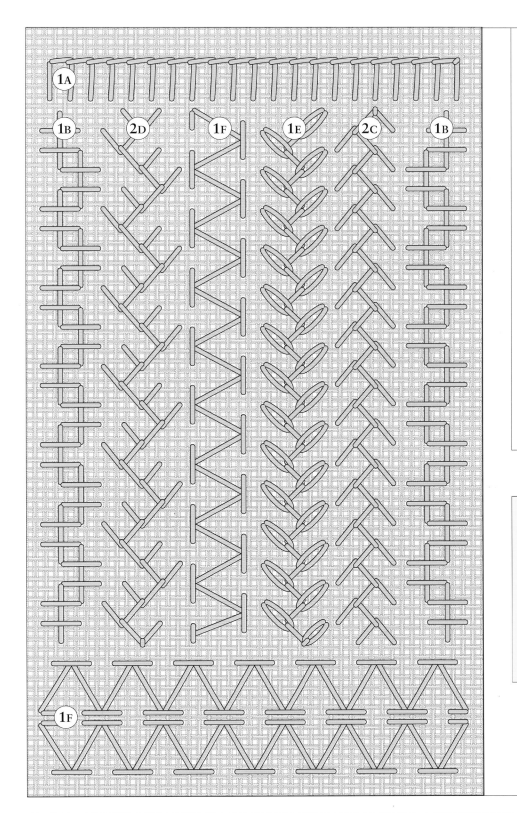

THREAD
1 Bond Multis
Springtime 07000-4
2 Anchor Marlitt
Lilac Pink 813

STITCHES
A Blanket Stitch
B Chinese Stitch
C Feather Stitch
D Double Feather Stitch
E Feathered Chain Stitch
F Chevron Stitch

STITCH NOTES
Work the blanket stitch,
Chinese stitch, chevron
stitch and feathered chain
stitch in Bond Multis. Work
the feather stitch and
double feather stitch rows
in Anchor Marlitt.

THREAD OPTIONS

Anchor Pearl Cotton
No. 5 can be used
instead of the Bond
Multis. As pearl
cotton is not variegated
you may wish to buy
a selection of
complementary
colours.

PROJECT TWO

EMBROIDERED TABLE SET

*T*his table mat, napkin and napkin ring make a delightful set and display your
ability with all three feather stitches. The table mat is embroidered with
double feather stitch, the napkin with feather stitch and the napkin ring with
feathered chain stitch. These items are so easy to stitch that you don't need a
chart – just follow the fabric grain or pattern to keep your stitching even.

YOU WILL NEED

Yellow cotton table mat(s)
51 x 40.5cm (20 x 16in) of cotton gingham with
  6mm (¹/₄in) checks for each napkin
20.5 x 13cm (8 x 5in) of cotton gingham with
  3mm (¹/₈in) checks for each napkin ring
Anchor Pearl Cotton No. 5 in brown 309
Milward crewel needle No. 6
Sylko cotton thread to match the gingham

1 If your table mat is ribbed you can use the rows
as a guide for the stitching, otherwise tack a set
of parallel lines 12mm (¹/₂in) apart to be your
stitching guide. Making sure you don't embroider
over the tacking, start at the top and work a line of
double feather stitches along the side of the mat
using one strand of Anchor Pearl Cotton in a
crewel needle. On completion remove the tacked
lines, if you used them, and lightly press on the
wrong side with a steam iron.

2 Make the napkin by turning each side of the
fabric over twice to form a 12mm (¹/₂in) hem;
machine stitch in place. Feather stitch along one
side with one strand of Anchor Pearl Cotton in a
crewel needle, using the checks as a stitching
guide. On completion lightly press on the wrong
side with a steam iron.

3 For the napkin ring use one strand of Anchor
Pearl Cotton in a crewel needle to stitch a row
of feathered chain stitches the length of the band,
using the checks as a guide. On completion fold
the band in half and machine stitch 12mm (¹/₂in)
from the edge to form a ring. Turn the ring inside
out and fold over the fabric at the top and
bottom so the band is 5cm (2in) wide. Overlap
the fabric and turn one edge under to form a
12mm (¹/₂in) hem; slipstitch to secure. Turn the
fabric out to reveal the finished napkin ring.
Repeat to make others as required.

PROJECT THREE

EMBROIDERED BAGS

*C*reate a decorative bag by embellishing striped or checked silk fabric with just one stitch – chevron stitch. It makes a fun accessory or a pretty gift bag. Choose thread colours which stand out well against the colours of your fabric. You don't need a chart – just follow the lines on the fabric with your stitching.

YOU WILL NEED
At least 33 x 21.5cm (13 x 8½in) of striped or
* checked silk sufficient to fit your frame*
Anchor Marlitt thread to complement your fabric
1m (1yd) of thin cord
Sylko cotton thread to match your fabric
Milward crewel needle No. 6
Stiletto or knitting needle for making eyelets
Carpet needle or sticky tape

1 Place the fabric in a frame – you can use either a roller frame or a large circular hoop (see pages 20-23).

2 Start stitching at the left-hand side and work rows of chevron stitches neatly from left to right to cover an area 28 x 16.5cm (11 x 6½in).

3 On completion remove the embroidery from the frame and lightly press it on the wrong side with a steam iron to remove any slight puckering. Fold the fabric in half and cut away surplus material, leaving a border of 12mm (½in) outside the embroidered area along the raw edges for seam allowances.

4 Machine stitch down the open side and across the bottom of the bag, taking a 12mm (½in) seam allowance. Silk frays badly, so finish the raw edges with pinking shears, zigzag stitch or oversewing. Fold over the fabric at the top of the bag twice by 6mm (¼in) to form a narrow double hem and secure with machine or hand stitches. If you wish you can decorate this hemmed edge with another line of chevron stitches in a contrasting colour.

5 Turn the bag right sides out and lightly press with a steam iron. Make eyelets 2.5cm (1in) from the top of the bag by inserting a stiletto or knitting needle at 12mm (½in) intervals. Take care not to damage the fabric. Thread the cord through the eyelets using a carpet needle or by wrapping a piece of sticky tape tightly around the end so you can thread it through like a shoe lace.

THREAD OPTIONS

Rayon threads look good on silk and synthetic materials, but if you intend stitching on cotton fabric you could use Stranded Embroidery Cotton or Anchor Pearl Cotton No. 5.

PROJECT FOUR

ORIENTAL VASE

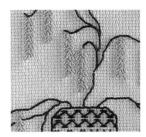

*A*lthough the stitches in this chapter are mainly used for decorative borders they can also be used to create pictures. This oriental vase is made up of a combination of border stitches: chevron stitch, feather stitch and Chinese stitch, while the catkins are created with short drops of feathered chain stitch.

YOU WILL NEED

At least 40.5 x 35.5cm (16 x 14in) of 11-count white Aida sufficient to fit your frame

Anchor Pearl Cotton No. 5 in yellow 302, brown 359 and blue 133

Milward tapestry and sharp or between needles

Frame with a 29 x 24cm (11½ x 9½in) aperture

Card for mounting to fit the frame

Drima extra-strong thread for lacing

Card mount to fit the frame with a 24 x 19cm (9½ x 7½in) oval aperture

Light-weight cotton fabric to cover the mount

Repositionable spray glue

Masking tape

1 Mount the Aida in a frame – a rectangular frame is best for a design of this size (see pages 20-23). For information on working from a chart see page 18.

2 Work the vase first following the chart on page 112 and using one strand of Anchor Pearl Cotton in a tapestry needle. Then stitch the stems in backstitch and the catkins in feathered chain stitch, also using one strand of thread.

3 On completion remove the embroidery from the frame and lightly press it on the wrong side with a steam iron.

4 Lace the work to the card (see page 28), and cover the mount with fabric (see page 29). Fit the laced embroidery behind the covered mount in the frame.

THREAD OPTIONS

Add extra sparkle to the catkins by stitching them with Anchor Marlitt or Bond Multis thread.

KEY

THREAD

ANCHOR PEARL COTTON NO. 5

1 Yellow 302
2 Brown 359
3 Blue 133

STITCHES

A Chinese Stitch
B Feather Stitch
C Chevron Stitch
D Blanket Stitch
E Feathered Chain Stitch
F Backstitch (page 31)

STITCH NOTES

The thread colour is indicated by a number and the stitch by a letter.

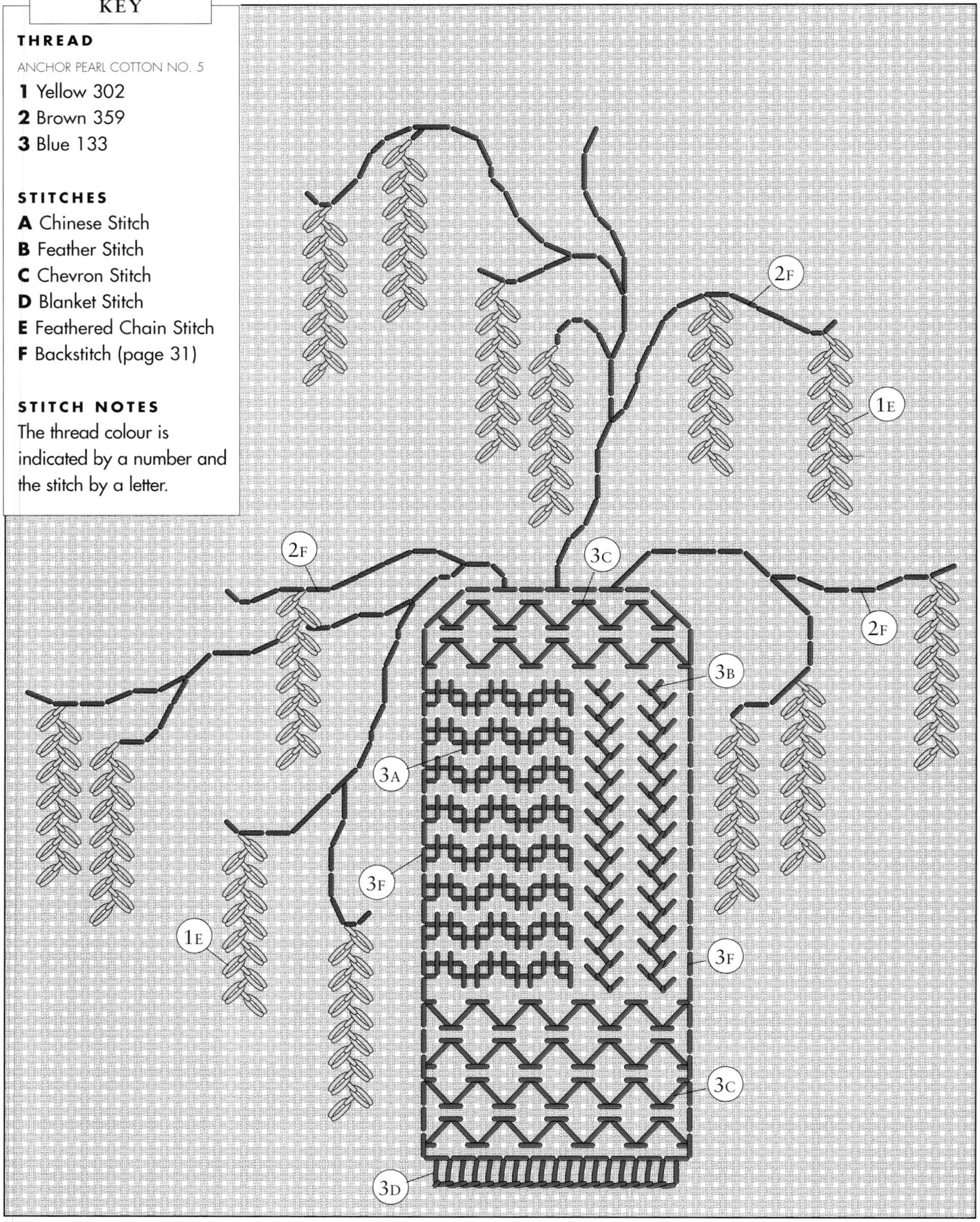

CHAPTER EIGHT

MIX & MATCH

hroughout this book options are given for each project, including suggestions for stitches, fabrics, threads, colours, repeat patterns and changes in project use. Here you can find out how to use these options to create your own individual embroideries.

CHANGING THE STITCH

You may wish to change a stitch for a number of reasons. For example, if you only have limited time to stitch, you might wish to consider using stitches from the outline family which are quick and easy to work. Perhaps you have enlarged a design and the suggested stitch is no longer appropriate – satin stitch, for example, which isn't suitable for covering a large area. Or it may simply be that you prefer one stitch to another.

Try working the same design in different stitches to see the effects. Refer to the Holly Christmas-tree Decorations (opposite) to find out how it's done.

CHANGING THE FABRIC AND THREADS

Most of the designs in this book are stitched on plain cotton because all the transfer methods work on this fabric and it is the easiest to stitch. However, although it is best to avoid stretchy, synthetic fabrics, you can use almost any fabric for embroidery.

For most fabrics you will require a light-weight cotton backing and for certain fabrics, such as felt, an iron-on interfacing is recommended. If you choose a synthetic or dark-coloured fabric you may also need to change your usual transfer method. The dressmakers' carbon and tacking methods are suitable for most fabrics (see pages 11-15).

Changing the threads can be both exciting and interesting: stitching with a mix of different threads can create an attractive assortment of textures. You can see this in action in the Floral Garlands (page 117).

When replacing one type of thread with another, use the chart at the top of this page as an approximate guide to strand numbers. The first column in the chart lists the thread types, the second column shows the number of strands each thread type has and the third column shows how many strands you would use to replace three strands of Anchor Stranded Cotton.

Thread	Number of strands in a skein	Replacement
Anchor Stranded Cotton	6 Strands	3 Strands
Anchor Marlitt thread	4 Strands	2 Strands
Anchor Pearl Cotton No. 5	1 Strand	1 Strand
Bond Multis	1 Strand	1 Strand

CHANGING THE COLOUR SCHEME

Changing a colour scheme is easy as long as you select colours in the same tonal range and follow the same pattern of shading as indicated in the original design. The tonal range refers to a selection of threads with the same colour density. If you wish to stitch a design in a soft colour scheme, for example, all the thread should be in pastel tones. When changing a colour scheme it is important that any shading in a design should remain the same, as illustrated by the Rose Pictures (page 120).

USING REPEAT PATTERNS

Repeat patterns are useful if you wish to use a motif as a design feature on a set of clothing or soft-furnishing items. A simple design can be repeated, rotated, enlarged, reduced or flipped. To flip a design, make a mirror image by simply using the front rather than the back of the tracing as a transfer – it's easy. You can try this out by making the complete Geranium Conservatory Set (see page 124).

ADAPTING DESIGNS

Most of the projects in this book can be adapted and used for another purpose. The Geranium Conservatory Set (page 124), for example, shows how the same motif can be used to produce cushions and pictures, or you could work a single motif on just about anything. When adapting a design for a different project take care to select suitable fabric and threads.

HOLLY CHRISTMAS-TREE DECORATIONS

*A*lthough it is fun to make your own Christmas-tree decorations, this is the sort of project that could be too time consuming – particularly because Christmas is a busy time of year. So this simple holly design has been stitched in three different ways to save on time and add extra interest to the decorations. The quickest design to make is worked in backstitch, while the satin stitch version takes the longest.

YOU WILL NEED

*At least 10cm (4in) square of felt sufficient
   to fit your frame*
*10cm (4in) square of light-weight iron-on
   interfacing*
*Anchor Stranded Cotton in red 46, light green
   256 and dark green 227*
Milward crewel needle No. 6
7.5cm (3in) star-shaped frame
Solid glue stick

1 Lay out the fabric right-side down. Place the interfacing glue-side down in the centre of the fabric and lightly press with a steam iron to fuse the layers together. Turn the fabric to the right side.

2 Transfer the design centrally to the fabric (see pages 11-15). A transfer pencil is best as it won't damage the surface of the felt.

3 Start the embroidery in the centre of the design using three strands of Anchor Stranded Cotton in a crewel needle.

4 On completion remove the embroidery from the frame and lightly press it on the wrong side with a steam iron. Place the star frame's cardboard backing over the embroidery, making sure the embroidery is centred, and draw round the card with a pencil. Check the design is correctly positioned, then trim away surplus fabric by cutting along the pencil line.

5 Spread a thin layer of glue from the solid glue stick onto the star-shaped card; place the fabric in position over the glued card and lightly press to secure it. Assemble the embroidery in the frame carefully following the manufacturer's instructions.

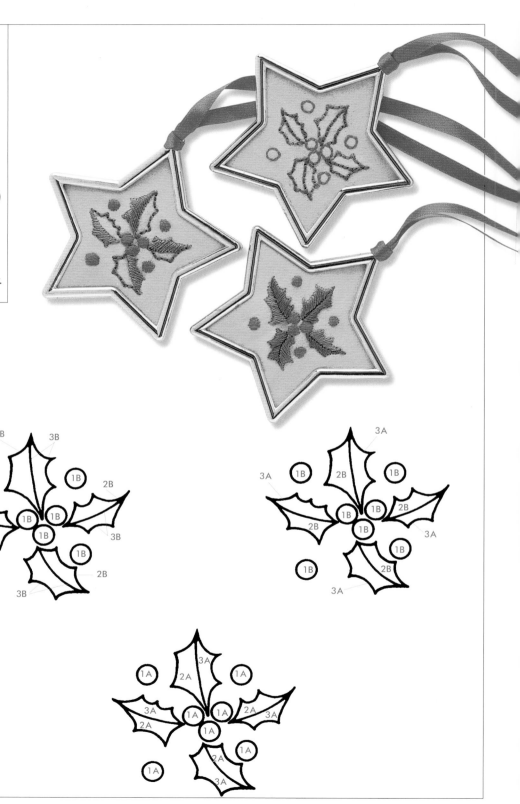

KEY

THREAD

ANCHOR STRANDED COTTON

1 Red 46
2 Light Green 256
3 Dark Green 227

STITCHES

A Backstitch (page 31)
B Satin Stitch (page 33)

STITCH NOTES

The thread colour is indicated by a number and the stitch by a letter.

PROJECT TWO

FLORAL GARLANDS

hese pretty floral garlands are stitched in a similar colour scheme on different fabrics and using different threads to show the effects these changes can make. One picture has been stitched using Anchor Stranded Cotton on two layers of light-weight cotton fabric and the other with a mix of different threads on synthetic fabric with a cotton backing.

YOU WILL NEED

At least 15cm (6in) square of light-weight cotton or synthetic fabric sufficient to fit your frame

Light-weight cotton backing the same size as your main fabric

Anchor Stranded Cotton or Anchor Pearl Cotton No. 5 and Anchor Marlitt thread as listed in the key on page 119

Milward crewel needle No. 6

10cm (4in) flexi-hoop

10cm (4in) square of white felt to finish the back of the frame

Sylko cotton thread in white for attaching the felt to the back of the mounted embroidery

1 Transfer the design to the fabric using one of the methods on pages 11-15. Mount the prepared fabric and backing together in a frame – you can either use an embroidery hoop or mount the fabric in your flexi-hoop (see pages 20-23).

2 Embroider the flowers first and then the leaves with the crewel needle. For the garland stitched in Anchor Stranded Cotton use three strands for all areas. For the mixed-thread garland use two strands of Anchor Marlitt thread for the flowers, one strand of Anchor Pearl Cotton for the flower centres and three strands of Anchor Stranded Cotton for the leaves.

3 On completion remove the embroidery from the frame and lightly press it on the wrong side with a steam iron.

4 If you have stitched the design in an embroidery hoop, trim off the excess fabric and mount the work in your flexi-hoop. If you have stitched the design in your flexi-hoop, trim the excess fabric to within 12mm (½in) of the frame. Gather in the fabric at the back and cover with felt (see page 30).

KEY

THREAD

ANCHOR STRANDED COTTON

1 Yellow 298
2 Red 79
3 Lilac 98
4 Violet 111
5 Green 226

ANCHOR PEARL COTTON NO. 5

6 Yellow 298

ANCHOR MARLITT THREAD

7 Red 815
8 Lilac 808
9 Violet 819

STITCHES

A Long-tailed Daisy
Stitch
B Lazy-daisy Stitch
C French Knot

STITCH NOTES
The thread colour is
indicated by a number
and the stitch by a letter.

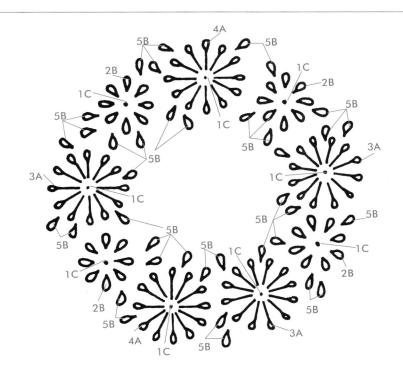

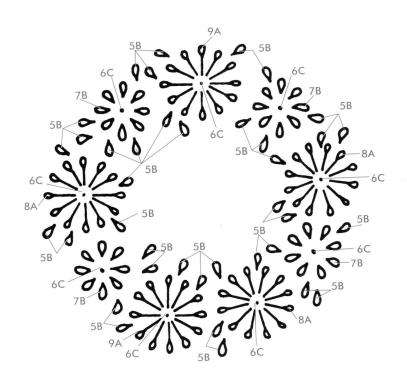

ROSE PICTURES

This lovely rose motif has been stitched in three different colourways to illustrate how you can change a colour scheme while retaining the shading. Three shades of one colour are used to stitch each rose. When the colour scheme is changed the lightest areas are still stitched with the lightest thread, and the darkest areas are replaced with the darkest thread.

YOU WILL NEED

At least 15 x 12.5cm (6 x 5in) of medium-weight white cotton fabric sufficient to fit your frame

Anchor Stranded Cotton in the colours given in the key

Milward crewel needle No. 6 and a sharp or between needle

8.5cm (3¼in) oval flexi-hoop

10cm (4in) square of white felt to finish the back of the frame

Sylko cotton thread to match the felt

1 Transfer the design to the fabric using one of the methods given on pages 11-15. A transfer pencil or soluble pen is ideal for a small design like this. Mount the prepared fabric in a frame – you can either use a circular hoop or mount the fabric in your flexi-hoop.

2 Start the embroidery in the centre of the fabric using three strands of Anchor Stranded Cotton in a crewel needle.

3 If you have stitched the design in an embroidery hoop, trim off the excess fabric and mount the work in the flexi-hoop. If you have stitched the design in your flexi-hoop, trim the excess to within 12mm (½in) of the frame. Gather in the fabric at the back and cover with felt (see page 30).

HANDY HINTS

Solid filling stitches are very prone to puckering, so even though this is a small design, make sure you secure your fabric firmly in your frame.

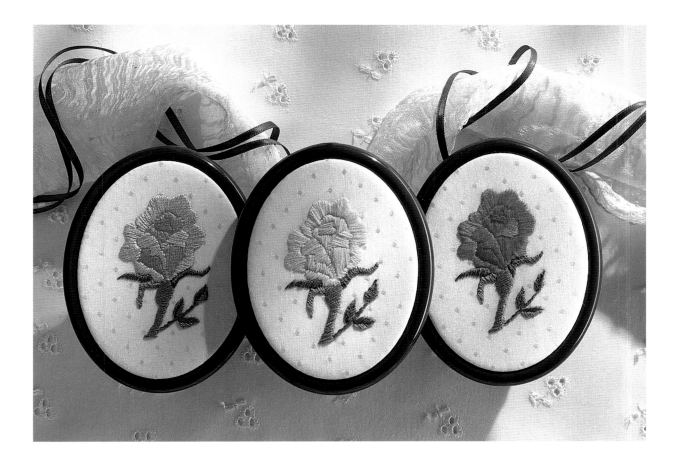

KEY

THREAD

ANCHOR STRANDED COTTON

YELLOW ROSE

1 Light Yellow 295
2 Medium Yellow 297
3 Deep Yellow 298
4 Light Green 226
5 Medium Green 227

PINK ROSE

1 Light Pink 50
2 Medium Pink 52
3 Deep Pink 54
4 Light Green 226
5 Medium Green 227

RED ROSE

1 Light Red 334
2 Medium Red 46

3 Deep Red 47
4 Light Green 226
5 Medium Green 227

STITCHES

A Satin Stitch (page 33)
B Stem Stitch (page 46)

STITCH NOTES

The thread colour is
indicated by a number
and the stitch by a letter.
The fine dotted lines
indicate the direction
of the stitch.

LAZY-DAISY DAYS

This simple but very pretty daisy design is used to decorate a pair of canvas shoes and a sun hat. The design is taken from Practice Sampler No. 1 (page 34) and worked in the same colours, but you can use different threads if you prefer. When selecting shoes for this project chose a pair with uppers made from a single layer of canvas, and use dressmakers' carbon to transfer the design. A transfer pencil is the best option for transferring the design to the hat band.

YOU WILL NEED

Canvas shoes

7.5cm (3in) wide strip of felt long enough to fit round your sun hat

Anchor Stranded Cotton in white 01, yellow 298 and green 243

Milward strong crewel needle No. 6 and a sharp or between needle

Sylko cotton thread to match the felt

Stiletto (optional)

Dressmakers' carbon and transfer pencil

1 Transfer the design onto each shoe using dressmakers' carbon (see page 14). Use a transfer pencil to transfer the design to the felt strip for the hat band (see page 13), spacing the daisies at regular intervals and rotating them as they travel along the band.

2 Stitch the design on the shoes using all six strands of Anchor Stranded Cotton in a strong crewel needle. If you have difficulty in pulling the needle through use a stiletto to pierce holes in the canvas as you stitch.

3 Stitch the design on the felt using all six strands of Anchor Stranded Cotton in a crewel needle. Take care not to damage the felt. On completion place the felt strip in position on the hat and slipstitch the two ends together to secure.

KEY

THREAD

ANCHOR STRANDED COTTON

1 White 01
2 Yellow 298
3 Green 243

STITCHES

A Backstitch
B French Knot
C Lazy-daisy Stitch

STITCH NOTES

The thread colour is indicated by a number and the stitch by a letter.

PROJECT FIVE

GERANIUM CONSERVATORY SET

*T*his richly coloured geranium motif is used to create a stylish set of mix-and-
match items for a conservatory. Three different cotton fabrics in the same
colourway are used to make all the items shown, including the mounts for
the pictures. On the cushions the design is stitched singly, as a flipped
image and as a repeat pattern. The pictures have been created
by stitching the design with one image flipped.

YOU WILL NEED

*Two squares at least 46cm (18in) of medium-
weight cotton fabric for each cushion sufficient
to fit your frame*

41cm (16in) cushion pad

*At least 30.5cm (12in) square of medium-weight
cotton fabric for each picture sufficient to fit
your frame*

*Anchor Stranded Cotton in bright red 46,
medium red 47, dark red 897, light green 266,
medium green 267 and dark green 268*

*19.5cm (7¾in) square of card for lacing for each
picture*

Drima extra-strong thread for lacing

19.5cm (7¾in) square frame for each picture

*19.5cm (7¾in) card mount with a 15cm (6in)
circular aperture*

*30.5cm (12in) square of plain medium-weight
fabric to cover the picture mount*

Sylko cotton thread to match the fabric

Milward crewel needle No. 6

Repositionable spray glue and masking tape

Solid glue stick

1 Transfer the design to the fabric using any of
the methods on pages 11-15. For the cushion
position the motif as desired; for the picture
centre the design. If you intend to make both
pictures, flip the image on one fabric so you have
a pair. Mount the fabric in a rectangular frame
(see pages 20-23).

2 Stitch all parts of the embroidery with three
strands of Anchor Stranded Cotton in a
crewel needle.

KEY

THREAD

ANCHOR STRANDED COTTON

1 Bright Red 46
2 Medium Red 47
3 Dark Red 897
4 Light Green 266
5 Medium Green 267
6 Dark Green 268

STITCHES

A Stem Stitch (page 46)
B Satin Stitch (page 33)

STITCH NOTES

The thread colour is indicated by a number and the stitch by a letter. The fine dotted lines indicate the direction of the stitch.

3 On completion remove the embroidery from the frame and lightly press it on the wrong side with a steam iron.

4 To make the cushion cover, pin the back and front together with right sides facing. Machine stitch round three sides taking a 12mm (½in) seam allowance. Snip the corners and turn the cover right sides out. Press it lightly. Slip the cushion pad inside, turn in the raw edges and slipstitch them together to finish.

5 To finish the picture, lace the work to the card (see page 28), then cover the mount with fabric (see page 29). Fit the laced embroidery and mount in the frame.

LIST OF SUPPLIERS

UK:
COATS CRAFTS UK
THE LINGFIELD ESTATES
MCMULLEN ROAD
DARLINGTON
COUNTY DURHAM
DL1 1YQ
TEL: +44 1 1325 365457

USA:
COATS AND CLARK
30 PATEWOOD DRIVE
SUITE 351
GREENVILLE
SC 29615
TEL: +1 864 234 0331

SOUTH AFRICA:
COATS SOUTH AFRICA (PTY) LTD
4 WOL STREET
HOMELAKE
PO BOX 347
RANDFONTEIN 1760
TEL: +27 11 693 5130

NEW ZEALAND:
COATS ENZED CRAFTS
46 LADY RUBY DRIVE
EAST TAMAKI
PO BOX 58-447
GREENMOUNT
AUKLAND
TEL: +64 9 274 7189

AUSTRALIA:
COATS PATONS CRAFTS
LEVEL 1
382 WELLINGTON ROAD
MULGRAVE
VICTORIA 3170
TEL: +613 9561 2288

CANADA:
COATS PATONS/COATS CANADA
INC.
1001 ROSELAWN AVENUE
TORONTO
ONTARIO
M6B 1B8
TEL: +1 416 782 4481

FRAMECRAFT MINIATURES LTD
372-376 SUMMER LANE
HOCKLEY
BIRMINGHAM
B19 3QA
TEL: 0121 212 0551

Index

NOTE: All illustration pages are shown in *italic*